P9-EGL-942

NEUROPSYCHOLOGICAL ASSESSMENT AND INTERVENTION WITH CHILDREN AND ADOLESCENTS

Lawrence C. Hartlage, PhD and Cathy F. Telzrow, PhD

Professional Resource Exchange, Inc.
Sarasota, Florida

Copyright © 1986 Professional Resource Exchange, Inc.
Professional Resource Exchange, Inc.
635 South Orange Avenue, Suites 4 & 5
Post Office Box 15560
Sarasota, FL 34277-1560

All rights reserved

No part of this book may be reproduced, stored in a
retrieval system, or transmitted, in any form or by any
means, either electronic, mechanical, photocopying,
microfilming, recording, or otherwise, without written
permission from the publisher.

Printed in the United States of America

Hardbound Edition ISBN: 0-943158-14-1
Paperbound Edition ISBN: 0-943158-15-X
Library of Congress Catalog Number: 86-70324

The copy editor for this book was Barbara Robarge, the
production supervisor was Debbie Worthington, the cover
designer was Bill Tabler, and the printer was McNaughton
& Gunn Lithographers.

"Let us now praise famous men, and our fathers that begat us."

(Ecclesiasticus, 44:1)

To **Clifton P. Hartlage** and **Leslie F. Fultz**, who taught by example the importance of developing character and setting goals, and the discipline for doing both. May the future be even fuller than the past.

TABLE OF CONTENTS

vi

PREFACE

This is a book for clinicians. While academicians and researchers may find the volume heuristically interesting, it is intended as a resource for psychologists who routinely evaluate and design educational and rehabilitation programs for children and adolescents with impaired neuropsychological functioning. With that purpose in mind, we attempted to present our assessment techniques and approaches to intervention in a direct, descriptive manner. In our experience, clinicians are immensely pragmatic people. We endeavored to respond to this by providing explicit details about test instruments and procedures, as well as how data may be integrated to generate hypotheses about neuropsychological functioning. Case studies were used liberally to illustrate the techniques described. We included tables of test instruments categorized by neuropsychological function, a list of the addresses of test publishers, and a glossary of terms in an effort to make our discussion as complete as possible. We hope that this specificity about test selection and interpretation, as well as the derivation of intervention strategies from assessment information, has produced a text that is relevant for graduate students, as well as practicing clinicians who may desire additional information before venturing into the sometimes perilous waters of pediatric neuropsychology.

A project such as this requires cooperation on many fronts, and we wish to acknowledge the assistance of those who contributed significantly to the development of this volume. First, we wish to thank our respective families, whose support and good humor through this and similar ventures is too seldom recognized. Second, we owe a significant debt to Professional Resource Exchange publishers Peter Keller and Larry Ritt. They conceptualized this volume and contributed in important ways to molding its character along the way. In addition, they managed all production steps in a remarkably efficient manner that was unusually painless and worry free for us as authors. And, most significantly, they have remained personally charming and supportive throughout the entire process. Peter and Larry: It has been a rare pleasure.

Finally, there are two populations that merit our special thanks. First, we salute practicing child clinicians, who ask astute questions, who cause us to stretch and experiment with new approaches, and who hold us to task when our suggestions are unrealistic or ineffective. And, most importantly, we wish to recognize the children, who teach us much and surprise us continually. It is our vast hope that this compilation of assessment and intervention strategies will contribute to maximizing their development.

1

INTRODUCTION TO NEUROPSYCHOLOGICAL ASSESSMENT AND INTERVENTION WITH CHILDREN

TRADITIONAL APPROACHES TO NEUROPSYCHOLOGICAL ASSESSMENT

It has long been apparent to professionals in such specialties as pediatrics, child psychiatry, and child psychology that children are not just small adults. Although the differences between children and adults are quite pronounced on such dimensions as reasoning, judgment, and causal attribution, such features as neuropsychological organization, functioning, and specialization show even greater variability between pediatric and adult populations. Nevertheless, for many years it has been accepted practice in child neuropsychology to utilize the same assessment strategies and measurement instruments that are used with adults.

A close look at the venerable Reitan-Indiana Neuropsychological Battery for Children, which represents a downward extension of the Halstead-Reitan Neuropsychological Battery found to be so sensitive to adult neuropathological conditions, contains many of the same measurement items, either with the more difficult items deleted (e.g., Categories Test) or with lowered normative expectations and pathognomonic cutoff scores (e.g., Finger Oscillation Test). A more recent child neuropsychological battery still in the experimental version, the Luria-Nebraska Neuropsychological Battery for Children, takes an even more direct approach to downscaling an adult battery by deleting those items from the (269 item) adult battery which normative research with children has indicated they are unlikely to perform.

The use of children's batteries based on adult models has typically focused on children from around ages 8 or 9 up to around age 14, with adult batteries considered appropriate after that age. There is some empirical support for using age 14 as an adult transition age, because from the earliest days of his original battery, Halstead determined that the mean item scores on most of his items were no different for children age 14 and above than for adults. From a conceptual point of view, however, there is reason to suspect that the sorts of judgment and other (presumably frontal lobe mediated) qualitative differences between young teenagers and mature adults are not measured adequately by the quantitative items on the Halstead-Reitan Battery, because full frontal lobe maturation may not be accomplished until late teen age for girls and possibly even later for boys.

For children under age 8 or 9, Reitan developed a special battery using a number of new test items, but this battery has not received the reception or widespread use achieved by his other batteries. Similarly, Golden and his co-workers at Nebraska have done a good deal of preliminary work with a younger children's battery, but validation work is still underway.

In terms of practical application, a standardized neuropsychological battery for children of elementary grade and preschool ages presents a number of technical and practical problems. Such issues as concentration, attention span, and motivation present limitations on strict standardization with a younger population. Further, the repertoire of measurable abilities with meaningful neuropsychological substrates decreases with age. As a result, considerable ingenuity, knowledge of child development expectancy levels for given abilities and their range of normal variability, and measurement sophistication, are added to the obvious requirement of neuropsychological expertise in the development of such a battery. Finally, since the cognitive development of the child covers such a wide range during ages from preschool to early elementary school years, a battery measuring the same abilities needs to have separate pass-fail criteria or levels required for pathognomonic significance at given ages. The well-known "spurts" and "plateaus" of child mental development represent examples of issues that can compound this latter consideration. Such variability requires special measurement expertise in developing confidence intervals that are at once sensitive to subtle problems and yet do not result in false positive classification errors.

LIMITATIONS TO THE
TRADITIONAL APPROACH

A number of neurologically related issues present formidable obstacles to the validation of neuropsychological assessment batteries with children. Whereas with adults it is often unfortunately easy to collect large sample data from victims of documented head injuries due to such wartime related problems as penetrating missile wounds, or from conditions often associated with advancing age, such as cerebrovascular accidents, with children such conditions are relatively rare. The localization or lateralization of brain insults from such causes is relatively easy with adults, given availability of neuroradiological reports, which can be correlated with neuropsychological battery data for validation of the battery against such criterion measures. Conversely, with children the sorts of brain insults that are most common, like those resulting from anoxia, intracranial infections, or mild closed head injury, are less likely to have neurosurgical validation and may have equivocal neuroradiological correlations. Thus in many cases the validation of neuropsychological batteries in children is based on less definitive criterion measures than are available for adults. Further, the age at which brain damage occurs in children may be much more related to the type or severity of neuropsychological impairment than in adults, which presents another impediment to validation of neuropsychological batteries with children.

A final problem with validation of neuropsychological batteries with children involves availability of normal controls for large sample normalization. With adults, a fairly large age range can be used for standardization: Adult age ranges of 20 or more years often are used as control populations. With children, especially younger children, differences of 2 or 3 years can require different measurement approaches or at least different normative data, so that many more controls are needed for validation. Further, captive control populations, such as college students enrolled in psychology courses, servicemen, hospitalized veterans, prisoners, and mental hospital patients, often have been used as controls in adult battery validation, whereas children are not so readily available from comparable sources.

In recognition of the problems inherent in attempting to do proper validation and standardization studies for child neuropsychological batteries, clinicians often have chosen other approaches to neuropsychological assessment of children. One approach involves the use of well standardized tests, in various combinations relative to the age and diagnostic questions involved for each child, in a flexible battery format. Such a procedure has the potential for addressing the diagnostic issue at hand with the most appropriate test battery. It does, however, require considerable neuropsychological sophistication on the part of the clinician, both with respect to choosing the tests most appropriate for specific diagnostic issues in a child of a given age, and with respect to making accurate diagnostic inferences based on test instruments that may vary in many aspects from child to child.

Perhaps the method of choice for most child neuropsychological clinicians involves the use of a more or less standard core battery of tests, which may be augmented by other special focus tests depending on the age of the child, the diagnostic issues in question, and areas suggested by the core battery as requiring greater elaboration or study. Because such an approach is the one preferred by most child clinical neuropsychologists, including the authors, this method is elaborated and exemplified in the third chapter, with additional discussion relative to the assessment of preschool children and adolescents contained in subsequent chapters.

BASIC PREMISES IN A NEUROPSYCHOLOGICAL MODEL OF ASSESSMENT

Before moving to a discussion of specific neuropsychological diagnostic approaches, it may be worthwhile to mention a few general conceptual premises underlying most approaches to neuropsychological assessment. These points will be discussed in greater detail in Chapter 3.

1. Central nervous system structures that develop neuroembryologically from the prosencephalon have contralateral (literally: "opposite side") representation. Thus with regard to the cerebral cortex, the left side of the brain controls the right side of the body for most motor and sensory functions.

2. In the overwhelming majority of right handers and the majority of left handers, the left cerebral hemisphere is more specialized for processing verbal and linguistic information content and for processing information in a logical, sequential, analytic manner.

3. Similarly, the right cerebral hemisphere is more specialized for processing spatial content, and for analyzing information in a simultaneous, holistic, gestalt manner.

4. Cerebral cortex structures just anterior to the Rolandic fissure (i.e., in the posterior portions of the frontal lobes) are related to motor functions, with contralateral representation. Thus the left cerebral hemisphere motor strip relates to movement of the right side of the body, and vice versa.

5. Cerebral cortex structures just posterior to the Rolandic fissure (i.e., in the anterior portion of the parietal lobes) are related to sensory and perceptual functions, with contralateral representation. Thus the left cerebral hemisphere sensory strip relates to sensation and perception of the right side of the body, and vice versa.

6. Even in very young children, the brain contains approximately 10 to 12 billion neurons, with more than 100 billion glial cells. Therefore terms like "brain injured" or "brain damaged" may not describe the individual's condition accurately. This lack of specificity is further compounded by the fact that damage to a very specific brain area may result in quite different effects, depending on such factors as age or sex of the child. It is rare that any two individuals would experience damage to the exact same area of the brain, with injury to the same number of neurons, at the same age and stage of neuromaturational development. Consequently, individuals with "brain injury" or

"brain   damage"   represent   an   extremely heterogenous group.

In addition to these general conceptual premises that can serve as guidelines for the interpretation of neuropsychological data, relatively independent of the battery or approach from which the data are obtained, there is an important baseline consideration to keep in mind.   More than 75% of all children have easily observable anatomic asymmetries of the brain, which are present even before birth and which persist throughout life.   To the extent that the structure of the brain is related to function of the brain, it is reasonable to expect some degree of functional asymmetry as representing the rule rather than the exception in neuropsychological organization.   Many psychometric tests have had the effects of this asymmetry partialled out by weighting procedures or the elimination of items that reflect this asymmetry.   However, on untreated measurement units such as grip strength, finger tapping rate, or direct measures of sensory or perceptual acuity, this asymmetry of function is more obvious.   The asymmetry is not equally represented in the two hemispheres, in that there is approximately 65% incidence of left hemispheric superiority over right, with only a 12% incidence of right over left hemispheric asymmetry.   Implications for such findings with regard to assessment of and intervention with children are described in Chapter 3.

With these premises and baseline data in mind, it is relevant to look at general considerations in neuropsychological assessment of children.   Such issues as early versus late brain insults, differentiation between developmental delay and impairment, and plasticity of the central nervous system, are particularly relevant when discussing the neuropsychology of pediatric populations. These and other topics are addressed in the following chapter.

2

GENERAL CONSIDERATIONS IN CHILD NEUROPSYCHOLOGICAL ASSESSMENT

A TRADITIONAL BATTERY VERSUS
A MODIFIED BATTERY APPROACH

As noted in Chapter 1, two general approaches to assessment are available to the child neuropsychologist or the child clinician who wishes to do some limited neuropsychological child assessment. The traditional approach, based on adult neuropsychological assessment methods, involves the use of a fixed battery with all patients. There are a number of clear advantages to such an approach. By using a battery that has been used by many others, there is some reassurance that it is probably a fairly appropriate neuropsychological assessment battery containing sufficient breadth and depth of items for comprehensive coverage. Additionally, there are likely to be norms based on a large number of cases and published data concerning profiles of test scores or configurations of responses that have been found to be common among given diagnostic groups. Further, the use of the same battery with every child makes it progressively easy to administer, score, and interpret data, because each test battery is an identical replication of the last. And finally, a standardized battery makes it comparatively easy to collect data, because such a procedure helps insure that essentially the same data are available for every child tested. Though not essential for clinical purposes, this potential for data accumulation may nevertheless be appealing to neuropsychologists who wish to use data from their evaluations for teaching, writing, or research purposes.

There are disadvantages to a fixed battery approach to neuropsychological assessment, and these drawbacks are especially manifest in child neuropsychological assessment. With respect to the mechanics of administration, a fixed battery assumes a certain homogeneity of abilities among examinees. Items must be sufficiently complex to avoid producing artificial ceiling effects among more gifted examinees, while extending downward to an extent that will measure functional levels with individuals of limited abilities, while not being so simplistic as to offend the more gifted. Among children in age ranges from beginning school to early adolescence, such homogeneity cannot be expected, even assuming there are not gifted or retarded children at upper and lower age ranges, respectively. In addition to the problems involving the range of mental abilities of children to be examined, the actual content needs to consider the effects of varied educational exposure usually related to differing ages. With adults, for example, it probably is safe to assume that most will have been exposed to the requirements for responding to questions like "Subtract 27 from 51." With younger school-aged children, however, even such apparently minor issues as whether letters are printed in capital or lower case depend on educational experience, with children in first grade more likely to give false positive pathognomonic answers to items in which part of the stimulus processing depends on recognition of the equivalence or meaning of letters. Similarly, a child who is the age of most third graders but who has been retained in first grade may appear to have "dyslexia," "dyscalculia," and other problems reflecting lower performance levels than are appropriate for his or her age level; they may, however, be appropriate to the level of academic exposure, even assuming adequate mental ability for third grade work.

Although a fixed neuropsychological battery for children might be developed to resolve methodological problems of the sort mentioned, it nevertheless may be inadequate for answering the questions or resolving the issues the testing was expected to accomplish. In the case of psychoeducational assessment for purposes of developing an individualized educational program (IEP), for example, a standardized neuropsychological battery like the Luria-Nebraska Children's Battery provides a great deal of information concerning the child's profile of strengths or deficits that may be relevant to psychoeducational planning; however, further measures such as IQ testing and achievement testing will be necessary for meeting requirements of the IEP. Further, a fixed neuropsychological battery is likely to represent an inefficient approach for resolving a number of referral issues, because it may sample many abilities that are irrelevant to a given referral question. For example, a good clinical history may reveal factors relevant to the diagnostic question and permit the neuropsychologist to focus a smaller number of tests toward developing a more comprehensive assessment of the suspected areas of dysfunction. A child with a history of dysphasia and right hemiparesis may not require a number of tests to determine whether he or she has a left cerebral hemisphere dysfunction; rather, an assessment of specific language and motor problems, along with items dealing with evaluation of residual strengths mediated by the intact cerebral hemisphere, may be more helpful in developing an appropriate management plan.

Finally, the setting in which a neuropsychologist functions may be a factor in determining the relevance of a fixed neuropsychological battery. Neuropsychologists in settings wherein little referral or background information concerning the child is available may be more comfortable with a fixed battery that will sample most higher cognitive functions and provide some safeguards against overlooking possible unsuspected problems. Conversely, if relevant neuroradiological (e.g., CT scan) or electrophysiological (e.g., EEG) data previously have determined presence, locus, or area of cortical dysfunction, a fixed battery may provide somewhat redundant information concerning these issues. When cost containment is a consideration, it may be difficult to justify the use of a fixed battery, because the comprehensiveness (and resultant time and costs involved) of a fixed battery normally will exceed the expenditures of time and money involved in an assessment approach directed toward more limited questions.

An approach to child neuropsychological assessment that incorporates both the comprehensiveness of a standard battery and the flexibility of an assessment designed to meet the special needs of each child is gaining in popularity and has a number of features that makes it attractive. The time involved is usually less than that required for a fixed battery, with resultant lowered demands for contact with the child and costs relative to examiner time. By assessing most relevant cortical areas and cognitive abilities in a briefer fashion, it permits additional focus on special findings that emerge from the testing, while helping insure that no significant aspects of function have been omitted from consideration. In addition, such an approach allows the introduction, as indicated, of special tests or subscales for assessment of unique issues that may be involved in the specific referral question.

An example of such a modified battery involves the use of (a) the age appropriate Wechsler scale, (b) sensory-perceptual assessment of such functions as recognition of numbers written on fingertips, (c) upper extremity motor evaluation of grip strength and rate of rapid finger oscillation, (d) achievement levels, (e) a measure of constructional praxis, (f) receptive language scale, and (g) a careful developmental and academic history. Then, depending on either the referral question or areas of interest that emerge from findings on the test items, additional special focus measures can be added. Because such an evaluation approach requires that the examiner have some frame of reference for thinking through findings and their possible implications, a conceptual approach to consideration of findings from such a diagnostic strategy may be of help in determining when such a modified battery may be appropriate.

DEVELOPMENTAL DELAY
VERSUS IMPAIRMENT

With respect to the differentiation among delay, dysfunction, or damage as possible etiologies in children's observed difficulties, if the purpose of the evaluation is developing an intervention program for the child, such differentiation may be unnecessary. In fact, making such distinctions may be irrelevant for practical purposes in many cases, if we can assume that the child has had adequate exposure to the sociocultural and educational environment, with sufficient opportunity for interaction with and development within that environment. Given that these experiences were provided for a number of years, with the developmental and examination data consistently favoring function of one side of the body over the other, the distinction among delay, dysfunction, and damage becomes academic with respect to its implication for intervention, planning, or programming. Conceptually, it may be appropriate to infer that dysfunction and even chronic delay may reflect damage. In an educational or social agency context, for example, where "damage" is required to make a child eligible for services, such an inference may be justifiable in some cases. In a medical or perhaps forensic context, where previous neurological (and perhaps neuroradiological and electrophysiological) examination has found no evidence of damage, neuropsychological findings may similarly support unilateral brain damage as an etiologic factor. However, in operational terms a more descriptive word such as dysfunction would more likely be used by the neuropsychologist. The term "delay," although compatible with the findings at a descriptive level, may be subject to optimism (especially by parents) with respect to the possibility that the child will eventually "outgrow" the problem.

Thus care needs to be exercised in the choice of terminology, ranging from descriptive (delay) to more inferential (dysfunction) to diagnostic (damage), even though all terms are often used by clinicians to describe findings based on similar configurations of data. If there is a positive medical history (e.g., unilateral seizures, hemiparesis), or very consistently large cognitive, motor, and sensory asymmetries (e.g., Verbal-Performance Wechsler discrepancies of 30 points, and 30% asymmetry between right- and left-hand function on sensory and motor measures, all in a compatible direction), then the term damage is, of course, more strongly supported by the findings, whereas in the absence of supportive medical history or strong asymmetry of function, the term dysfunction may be preferred.

With respect to the nature or type of delay, dysfunction, or damage, hypotheses generated from the findings can be tested further by additional questioning. Such issues as possible similar patterns in other family members occasionally may be relevant, especially among males, because there is long-standing recognition that certain functional abilities may be transmitted as gene loci on the X chromosome (Corah, 1965; Hartlage, 1970; Lehrke, 1972; Stafford, 1961). Further, the incidence of anatomic cerebral asymmetry in presumably "normal" individuals appears to be in the range of 77%, especially involving the upper surfaces of the temporal lobe and the area lying between Heschl's gyrus and the posterior margin of the Sylvian fossa (Galaburda, LeMay, Kemper, & Geschwind, 1978; Geschwind & Levitsky, 1968), with anatomic asymmetries observable before birth (Chi, Dooling, & Gilles, 1977). Thus it is important to keep in mind, especially in cases involving comparatively small magnitudes of asymmetry, the possibility of what may be normal variation in levels of function related to anatomic cerebral asymmetry.

Because many childhood acquired neuropsychological disorders, such as those involving toxicity, anoxia, or intracranial hemorrhage, are prenatal or perinatal in origin, the sequelae of such acquired insults to the central nervous system would present as chronic. Even among children at high risk for such problems, there is considerable variability in functional outcome among children with specific documented perinatal disorders (Hartlage & Telzrow, 1982a), so that in many cases it is difficult to establish a specific insult that will account for findings.

Finally, recent conceptualizations concerning genotype-environment relationships (Scarr & McCartney, 1983) suggest that individuals with genotypic strengths in given ability clusters may tend to seek out (and resultantly become more proficient in) stimuli and activities compatible with these strengths. As a consequence, a child with early determined functional assets might develop proportionally greater facility over time in functions related to these strength areas, producing, in effect, an enhancement of functional asymmetry by increased performance of tasks dependent on these abilities, while showing progressive decline on performance of tasks mediated by areas of underlying weakness. Follow-up of children with school learning problems tends to support this concept (Williams, Hartlage, Noonan, & Prim-Power, 1983), thus raising the possibility that manifestations of functional cerebral asymmetry, although obviously related to neuropsychological substrates, may in fact represent a relatively complex phenomenon. Accordingly, careful questioning concerning preferred activities, school subjects, and styles of learning and performance may help clarify the interactions of these variables as they relate to a given child's profile.

EARLY VERSUS LATE INSULT

For a number of years, it has been believed that there is better likelihood of recovery from early age as opposed to later age onset of brain lesions (Black, Jeffries, Blumer, Wellner, & Walker, 1969; E. H. Lenneberg & E. Lenneberg, 1975). This belief has been supported by research showing greater sparing of language and more rapid recovery from acquired aphasia in young children (Alajouanine & Lhermitte, 1965; Hecaen, 1976; Levin & Eisenberg, 1979; St. James-Roberts, 1979), and a lower mortality rate after severe head injury in children than in adults (Bruce, Schut, Bruno, Woods, & Sutton, 1978; Hendrick, Harwood-Hash, & Hudson, 1964). Accumulating research, however, has suggested that young children may demonstrate as much or even more neurocognitive impairment from brain injury than older children and adults who suffer the same type and severity of head injury (Brink, Garrett, Hale, Woo-Sam, & Nickel, 1970; Kleinpeter, 1976; Levin, Benton, & Grossman, 1982). Aram, Ekelman, Rose, and Whitaker (1985) reported that verbal and cognitive sequelae following unilateral lesions acquired early in childhood follow a pattern similar to those acquired at later ages, and Satz (1985) and his co-workers (Orsini, Satz, & Soper, 1985) found that early onset is associated with greater global cognitive decline than later onset. Compatible findings with identical twins were reported by Lyons and Matheny (1984). Levin, Eisenberg, Wigg, and Kobayashi (1982) found equal or more severe consequences of brain injury due to closed head injury in children when compared with adolescents, and Cermak (1985) found that, in addition to head injury, infectious and metabolic brain insults were also more likely to result in severe impairments in younger than in older children.

The specific age that separates "younger" from "older" children with respect to neuropsychological sequelae of brain injury is not clear, partly because different investigators use different cutoff ages. Satz and his co-workers, for example, use 6 years to differentiate between younger and older children. Lyons and Matheny reported findings for children under versus over 36 months, Kleinpeter studied a group ranging up to 15 years of age, and Brink, Garrett, Hale, Woo-Sam, and Nickel used 8 years as their dividing point. Other investigators (Lange-Cosack, Wilder, & Schlesener, 1979) separated infants and toddlers from preschool and kindergarten-age children and reported greater cognitive sequelae in the younger group. Although the critical age for maximum impairment from brain injury is not clear, there is controlled research to suggest that brain injury at younger ages, however defined, may produce greater impairment than injury sustained at later ages.

CENTRAL NERVOUS SYSTEM (CNS) PLASTICITY

It is recognized that the behavioral consequences of damage to the central nervous system change as the time following injury increases (Marshall, 1984). The interpretation of this change can be either on the basis of normalization of function or as a manifestation of CNS plasticity. Since early in the past century, recovery from brain injury has been reported in experimental animals (Flourens, 1824), prompting a number of explanations to account for the phenomenon.

One popular explanation involves the development of new strategies for coping with lost abilities, more or less independent of any CNS regeneration or plasticity. Another explanation, similarly independent of CNS plasticity, involves the considerable redundancy in the central nervous system, so that even if a sizable number of neurons are damaged, there are a sufficient number remaining to permit the performance of a given behavior.

Recent work in such areas as axonal sprouting has tended to support CNS plasticity as an explanation, although the actual mechanisms involved or their susceptibility to modification or rehabilitation remains unclear. Two major theoretical approaches account for most plasticity explanations. One theory suggests that structural changes occur in the brain due to axonal and dendritic proliferation, so that actual regeneration accounts for improvement in behavior. The other theory proposes that neurons near the site of injury become more responsive to neurotransmitters, and thus account for improvement by means of neurochemical adaptation.

Although each of the explanations, whether involving alternative strategies, redundancy, structural regrowth, or neurochemical adaptation, is supported by considerable research, none accounts for findings that early age brain injury is more handicapping than later age brain injury. Perhaps of more immediate consequence, none offers any specific and proven guidelines for enhancing recovery of function following CNS injury. Interestingly, a finding associated with optimal behavioral outcome in very young children suffering CNS damage in the perinatal period is not related to any of these explanations. Follow-up of a fairly large sample of children suffering a variety of CNS insults at or around birth revealed that an enriched, stimulating environment is associated with best prognosis for good mental progress after about age 2 (Hartlage, 1981b), although the mechanism underlying this finding is not at all clear.

From a clinical perspective, based on observations of children of varying ages over several years following CNS insult, in many cases both the child and the child's family make some modifications in their expectancies and approaches to cognitive tasks. Thus what appears to be "improvement" may, in many cases, represent a scaling down of parental expectations for the child, and the child's learning to avoid attempting tasks on which frustration or failure is likely.

ENVIRONMENTAL INTERACTIONS
WITH CNS IMPAIRMENT

The child with CNS impairment may be expected to have experiences which differ in some ways from those of children with intact CNS function. Whether the CNS impairment involves motor, visual, auditory, or other functions, care must be taken in the interpretation of findings according to strict actuarial criteria, because altered environmental interactions related to CNS dysfunction may make such interpretation spurious.

Two factors necessitate special care in the interpretation of test findings for children with CNS impairment. One factor involves a tendency toward compensation, whereby the child tends to focus efforts on tasks or approaches to tasks that are more likely to be successful. Over a half century ago, for example, psychologists noted that blind children appear to become more skillful in listening, to the point where they surpass sighted peers on such abilities (S. C. Pressey & L. W. Pressey, 1918; Terman, 1916). With milder impairments, there is a similar tendency for the child to focus on tasks that he or she can perform, and this can result in a comparatively uneven profile of test scores. In the case of mild receptive dysphasia, as in a language learning disorder, heightened attention to (and corresponding enhanced facility with) visual details is common, and may be reflected in such areas as comparatively high levels of performance on tests involving picture completion or visual closure, or in meticulous execution of drawing and copying tests.

The other factor requiring caution in the interpretation of test results for children with CNS impairment involves the fact that children tend to avoid tasks or approaches to problem solving on which their CNS impairment presents them with difficulty. In a clinical testing situation, the child with the sort of receptive dysphasia just mentioned may diligently and enthusiastically perform on nonverbal tasks, compared with his or her withdrawal from or comparatively poorer effort on language-related test items. On the Wechsler Intelligence Scale for Children-Revised (WISC-R) subtests, for example, such a child may make comments like "Let's do some more pictures" (i.e., Picture Completion) when the examiner moves to a more verbally mediated subtest like Similarities. The chronic avoidance of tasks on which CNS impairment makes good performance difficult thus serves to provide an accumulative impairment, consisting of both the limitations imposed by the CNS impairment and the lack of practice via experiential interaction with the specific tasks.

Because of the likelihood of accumulative impairment (and corresponding compensation), there is a tendency for children with CNS impairments to show greater discrepancies between performance on comparative strength and deficit tasks over time. This can lead to false positive estimates of deterioration of the child's underlying CNS function. In the case of a child with mild cerebral palsy, for example, the developmental psychomotor activities assumed for a child without CNS impairment are assumed in the normative expectancy tables for performance at given ages. Thus on items requiring psychomotor development and coordination, such as design copying or WISC-R Object Assembly, with increasing age the child with mild cerebral palsy may fall progressively below age expectancy compared to a child without such experiential limitations. This may suggest a decline in the integrity of the child's psychomotor ability or, by inference, in the integrity of the CNS function underlying such ability.

Because of the substantial variation on effect of limited environmental interaction relative to such factors as type, severity, age at onset of CNS impairment, and age at testing, and each child's unique ways of coping with such impairment, it is not feasible to establish definitive or even general guidelines for estimating effects of such impairment on given test scores. However, whether the impairment be a neurologically documented one, such as cerebral palsy, dysphasia, or spatial dysfunction, or a milder, functional variant that might occur from lateralized cerebral asymmetry, the effects of environmental interactions with the underlying CNS impairment or limitation need to be considered in the interpretation of findings.

THE FLEXIBLE ASSESSMENT APPROACH

The neuropsychological assessment of some children for whom fairly specific questions are at issue is often approached by the use of a unique array of tests that may be different for each child. This assessment approach may miss some neuropsychological impairments that are present and amenable to detection and that also have relevance to the referral question. It further imposes considerable demands on the clinician to have knowledge of and proficiency with a fairly wide variety of tests and other assessment procedures, many of which may be used only occasionally for specific referral questions. In some settings, however, such an approach offers a relatively efficient strategy for answering questions related to specific aspects of function.

For example, in settings where a pediatrician, child neurologist, or child psychiatrist wishes to evaluate neuropsychological effects of methylphenidate (Ritalin) on children's behavior and learning, an abbreviated battery that directs attention to measures relevant to these phenomena may represent the most efficient approach. Presumably, such children already have had some previous diagnostic evaluation, perhaps oriented toward the establishment of a diagnosis of attention deficit disorder, possibly with hyperactivity. Thus the focus is not directed toward comprehensive neuropsychological diagnosis so much as toward discrete measures presumably attributable to the drug (Hartlage & Telzrow, 1982b). In such instances, tests of attention; attention span; concentration; short, intermediate, and long-term memory; behavior; and activity level normally will be sufficient to answer the specific question at issue, but may well miss such possible contributory factors as prior head trauma, incipient cerebral neoplasm, or birth injury.

Even in some neurological settings, more specific and limited special focus diagnostic approaches may be used. Such questions as the possible effects of varying therapeutic level serum concentrations of given anticonvulsant medications on the child's adaptive abilities can be approached with a limited array of tests that have maximal sensitivity to phenomena likely to be related to such intervention (Hartlage, 1981a). Again, use of a limited array of tests is done in the context of a previous diagnosis (i.e., epilepsy). Although it may produce neurobehavioral sequelae that can influence some aspects of test results, it represents a classificatory rather than comprehensive diagnostic procedure, and the focus of the referral question is quite limited.

It is apparent in the previous two examples that the role of neuropsychological assessment described here is quite different from one in which it is oriented toward a primary diagnostic role. Such assessment can be of considerable value for answering limited types of questions but is not adequate for a free-standing evaluation of neuropsychological function. For such purposes, neuropsychologists who do not use a formal (e.g., Reitan-Indiana or Luria-Nebraska Children's) neuro-psychological battery or a modified battery that uses at least screening measures of most cortical areas or functional systems, tend to assemble various combinations and permutations of assessment measures that they consider appropriate and adequate for addressing either the specific diagnostic issue for each child, or that are compatible with the typical referral questions with which they are faced. In a survey of practicing neuro-psychologists, Hartlage and Telzrow (1980) found that slightly more than a third used the full Reitan Battery, and slightly fewer than a third used the full Luria Battery, with approximately 89% using the Wechsler Intelligence Scales, 56% using portions of the Reitan Battery, 52% using the Wide Range Achievement Test, and 49% using the Bender Gestalt Test. Other tests used included the Benton Visual Retention Test (32%); the Wechsler Memory Scale (14%); the Graham Kendall Memory for Designs Test (9%); Projective Measures (7%); and (under 5%) the Boston Aphasia Examination, Raven Matrices, Illinois Test of Psycholinguistic Abilities, Peabody Picture Vocabulary Test, and Beery Test of

Visual Motor Integration, with many other tests used by smaller percentages of respondents. Subsequent studies of other neuropsychologists (Hartlage, 1985; Hartlage, Chelune, & Tucker, 1981) have resulted in essentially similar findings. Although the surveys did not differentiate between child and adult assessment, findings suggest that there does not appear to be a simple diagnostic battery that represents the standard of practice in neuropsychological assessment for either adults or children.

SUMMARY

The choice of assessment approaches represents an important consideration in child neuropsychological assessment. For many years a standardized battery approach represented the accepted procedure, and there is still considerable sentiment that such an approach represents the best assessment procedure. Although there are a number of factors that recommend the use of a standard battery for all children (e.g., comprehensiveness, standardization), there are also a number of limitations (e.g., redundancy; cost of child and examiner time; lack of responsiveness to each child's unique referral issue) that have caused many neuropsychologists to adopt other approaches.

For those who choose other approaches, the most common procedure is to use a small core battery of essentially the same test for all children, and augment this small battery with other more specialized tests or data as indicated by either the referral question or findings from the core battery. In some cases, a unique battery for each given diagnostic category, or each individual child, may be indicated. Although these approaches require considerable examiner skill, sophistication, and flexibility, they permit direct focus on each child and a unique diagnostic question, thus allowing sensitivity to the issues for which a given child is being evaluated. Different assessment approaches may be more or less useful in different settings, and all three approaches (standard battery, flexible battery, individualized assessment) may be appropriate in a given setting for addressing certain issues or questions.

REFERENCES

Alajouanine, T., & Lhermitte, F. (1965). Acquired aphasia in children. *Brain, 88,* 653-662.

Aram, D. M., Ekelman, B. L., Rose, D. F., & Whitaker, H. A. (1985). Verbal and cognitive sequelae following unilateral lesions acquired in early childhood. *Journal of Clinical and Experimental Neuropsychology, 7,* 55-78.

Black, P., Jeffries, J., Blumer, D., Wellner, A., & Walker, A. (1969). The post-traumatic syndromes in children. In A. Walker, W. Caveness, & M. Critchley (Eds.), *Late Effects of Head Injury* (pp. 142-149). Springfield, IL: C. C. Thomas.

Brink, J. D., Garrett, A. L., Hale, W. R., Woo-Sam, J., & Nickel, V. L. (1970). Recovery of motor and intellectual functions in children sustaining severe head injuries. *Developmental Medicine and Child Neurology, 12,* 565-571.

Bruce, D. A., Schut, L., Bruno, L., Woods, J. H., & Sutton, L. N. (1978). Outcome following severe head injury in children. *Journal of Neurosurgery, 48,* 679-688.

Cermak, L. A. (1985, February). *The Effects of Age at Onset and Causal Agent of Brain Injury on Later Adaptive Functioning in Children* (Abstract in Proceedings, p. 10). Paper presented at International Neuropsychological Society, San Diego.

Chi, J. G., Dooling, E. C., & Gilles, F. H. (1977). Gyral development of the human brain. *Annals of Neurology, 1,* 86-93.

Corah, N. C. (1965). Differentiation in children and their parents. *Journal of Personality, 33,* 300-308.

Flourens, P. (1824). *Recherches Experimentales sur les Proprietes, et les Fonctions du Systeme Nervoux dans les Animaux Vertebres.* Paris: Chez Crevat.

Galaburda, A. M., LeMay, M., Kemper, T. L., & Geschwind, N. (1978). Right-left asymmetries of the brain. *Science, 199,* 852-856.

Geschwind, N., & Levitsky, W. (1968). Human brain: Left-right asymmetries in temporal speech region. *Science, 161,* 186-187.

Hartlage, L. C. (1970). Sex-linked inheritance of spatial ability. *Perceptual and Motor Skills, 31,* 610.

Hartlage, L. C. (1981). Neuropsychological assessment of anticonvulsant drug toxicity. *Clinical Neuropsychology, 3,* 20-22. (a)

Hartlage, L. C. (1981, October). *Neurological Sequelae of Perinatal Insult.* Paper presented at National Academy of Neuropsychologists meeting, Orlando. (b)

Hartlage, L. C. (1985, August). *Past, Present, and Emerging Trends in Clinical Neuropsychology.* Paper presented at American Psychological Association meeting, Los Angeles.

Hartlage, L. C., Chelune, G., & Tucker, D. (1981, August). *Survey of Professional Issues in the Practice of Clinical Neuropsychology.* Paper presented at American Psychological Association meeting, Anaheim.

Hartlage, L. C., & Telzrow, C. F. (1980). The practice of clinical neuropsychology in the U. S. *Clinical Neuropsychology, 2,* 200-202.

Hartlage, L. C., & Telzrow, C. F. (1982). Specific medical findings which predict specific learning outcomes. In W. Cruickshank & J. Lerner (Eds.), *Coming of Age* (Vol. 3, the best of ACLD, pp. 36-44). Syracuse, NY: Syracuse University Press. (a)

Hartlage, L. C., & Telzrow, C. F. (1982). Neuropsychological disorders in children: Effects of medication on learning and behavior. *Journal of Research and Development in Education, 15,* 55-65. (b)

Hecaen, H. (1976). Acquired aphasia in children and the ontogenesis of hemispheric functional specialization. *Brain and Language, 3,* 114-134.

Hendrick, E. B., Harwood-Hash, D. C. F., & Hudson, A. R. (1964). Head injuries in children: A survey of 4465 consecutive cases at the Hospital for Sick Children, Toronto, Canada. *Clinical Neurosurgery, 11,* 46-59.

Kleinpeter, U. (1976). Social integration after brain trauma during childhood. *Acta Paedopsychiatrica, 42,* 68-75.

Lange-Cosack, H., Wilder, B., & Schlesener, J. H. (1979). Prognosis of brain injuries (one until five years of age). *Neuropaediatrie, 10,* 105-127.

Lehrke, R. (1972). A theory of X-linkage of major intellectual traits. *American Journal of Mental Deficiency, 76,* 611-619.

Lenneberg, E. H., & Lenneberg, E. (1975). *Foundations of Language Development: A Multidisciplinary Approach.* New York: Academic Press.

Levin, H. S., Benton, A. L., & Grossman, R. G. (1982). *Neurobehavioral Consequences of Closed Head Injury.* New York: Oxford University Press.

Levin, H. S., & Eisenberg, H. M. (1979). Neuropsychological impairment after closed head injury in children and adolescents. *Journal of Pediatric Psychology, 4,* 389-402.

Levin, H. S., Eisenberg, H. M., Wigg, N. R., & Kobayashi, K. (1982). Memory and intellectual ability after head injury in children and adolescents. *Neurosurgery, 11,* 668-672.

Lyons, M. J., & Matheny, A. P. (1984). Cognitive and personality differences between identical twins following skull fracture. *Journal of Pediatric Psychology, 9,* 485-494.

Marshall, J. F. (1984). Brain function: Neural adaptations and recovery from injury. *Annual Review of Psychology, 35,* 277-308.

Orsini, D. L., Satz, P., & Soper, H. V. (1985, August). *Cognitive Development Following Early Brain Injury.* Paper presented at American Psychological Association meeting, Los Angeles.

Pressey, S. C., & Pressey, L. W. (1918). A group point scale for measuring general intelligence. *Journal of Applied Psychology, 2,* 250-269.

Satz, P. (1985, August). *Recovery from Early Brain Damage: Some Facts and Reflections.* Paper presented at American Psychological Association meeting, Los Angeles.

Scarr, S., & McCartney, D. (1983). How people make their own environments: A theory of genotype-environment effects. *Child Development, 54,* 424-425.

Stafford, R. E. (1961). Sex differences in spatial visualization as evidence of sex-linked inheritance. *Perceptual and Motor Skills, 13,* 428.

St. James-Roberts, I. (1979). Neurological plasticity recovery from brain insult, and child development. *Advances in Child Development and Behavior, 14,* 253-319.

Terman, L. M. (1916). *The Measurement of Intelligence.* Boston: Houghton Mifflin.

Williams, D., Hartlage, L., Noonan, M., & Prim-Power, J. (1983, August). *Observations on Re-Evaluation of Children for Special Class Placement.* Paper presented at American Psychological Association annual meeting, Anaheim.

3

LEARNING DISABILITIES: ASSESSMENT AND INTERVENTION WITH SCHOOL-AGED CHILDREN

DEFINITION AND ILLUSTRATION OF LEARNING DISABILITIES

This chapter addresses various chronic, often quite subtle neuropsychological disorders that generally are referred to as *learning disabilities* (LD). The term may be a confusing one because the expression of learning disabilities varies considerably among individuals. Furthermore, definitions of learning disabilities tend to be imprecise and subjective, and diverse agencies (e.g., educational agencies and health care providers, such as hospitals or clinicians in private practice) often use different criteria for the identification of learning disabilities in their pediatric populations.

As a general working definition, we support the one adopted in 1985 by the Association for Children and Adults with Learning Disabilities:

Specific Learning Disabilities is a chronic condition of presumed neurological origin which selectively interferes with the development, integration, and/or demonstration of verbal and/or non-verbal abilities.

Specific Learning Disabilities exists as a distinct handicapping condition in the presence of average to superior intelligence, adequate sensory motor systems, and adequate learning opportunities. The condition varies in its manifestations and in degree of severity.

23

Throughout life the condition can affect self-esteem, education, vocation, socialization, and/or daily living activities. ("ACLD Offers New Definition," 1985, pp. 1, 19)

This definition communicates several important features that are characteristic of learning disabilities. Of primary importance is the assumption that learning disabilities are associated with neurologic dysfunction, which, although not observable on such hard neurological data sources as electroencephalogram (EEG) (McCauley & Ciesielski, 1982) and computerized axial tomography (CT) scan (Denckla, LeMay, & Chapman, 1985), are nevertheless apparent on more sensitive neuropsychological measures. Second, this definition reflects the chronicity of neurologically based learning disabilities. In the past it was assumed, particularly in the field of special education, that learning disabilities could be remediated or outgrown. Now we generally recognize that this is not the case. Although individuals with learning disabilities may, with specialized training and hard work, learn to circumvent or compensate for their observed problems, the underlying neuropsychological dysfunction remains. A third important characteristic of learning disabilities that is reflected in this definition is the often pervasive and devastating nature of the condition.

We recognize that the expression of learning disabilities may be "general" or "specific." The term "general learning disabilities," as used here, refers to a subtle disorder of attention and concentration typically referred to as "attention deficit disorder" or ADD syndrome. "Specific learning disabilities" (or SLD), as the name implies, are reflected in a specific and discrete disruption of language-related skills such as speaking, reading or writing, or mathematics. Within these two major categories are further subtypes of disorders. Attention deficit disorders, for example, may be expressed with or without hyperactivity. Subtypes of specific learning disabilities include dyslexia and dysgraphia. Each of these will be discussed in greater detail in subsequent sections of this chapter. Learning disabilities also can be described on a severity continuum ranging from mild to severe.

We wish to emphasize once again that historically the diagnosis of learning disabilities has been characterized by subjectivity and imprecision. In practice, one professional may identify a mildly distractible youngster as learning disabled, while another more conservative clinician may categorize such behavior as within normal limits. The issue of definition becomes most critical within the context of an educational agency, because identification of a child as learning disabled must precede eligibility for special education services. With rare exceptions, special education for learning disabled children is limited to those who have specific learning disabilities as outlined under federal law. Hence, children with ADD alone probably would not be eligible for such services unless it can be demonstrated that the attention deficit has severely interfered with achievement in one or more of the basic achievement areas. Furthermore, because special education in all states is funded almost exclusively by Education of the Handicapped monies, which prescribe that services are reserved for those with the most severe needs, we advocate utilization of this severity criterion in the identification of specific learning disabilities in the public schools. While the term might be used by clinicians to help parents, teachers, and children understand unique difficulties experienced in certain subject areas, we do not advocate use of the handicapped label and special education services for children with mild expressions of the disorder.

ATTENTION DEFICIT DISORDER

The formal definition of attention deficit disorder is taken from the *Diagnostic and Statistical Manual* (3rd ed.), of the American Psychiatric Association (1980). The condition may be expressed either with or without hyperactivity. In the latter, children may exhibit depressed scores on tests requiring attention and concentration, such as the Arithmetic, Digit Span, and Coding subtests of the WISC-R. In the classroom they may have difficulty following directions and may seek clarification and teacher assistance. Independent work habits may be poor, and they may not be able to complete a task successfully without considerable teacher encouragement. The first case study later in this chapter illustrates attention deficit disorder without hyperactivity.

Children who exhibit attention deficit disorders with hyperactivity are generally much easier to identify. In addition to the behaviors described above, such children may fidget constantly, moving in their chairs from a sitting position to kneeling on the floor or seat, to standing, leaning over their desks. They may leave their seats frequently, ostensibly for legitimate purposes, such as sharpening pencils or throwing away bits of paper. They may chatter out loud or mumble or sing to themselves. In addition to evidence of distractibility on the WISC-R, as described above, their scores on behavior rating scales such as the Connors (Connors, 1969, 1982) or the parent or teacher version of the Child Behavior Checklist (Achenbach & Edelbrock, 1983) are frequently elevated on the hyperactivity dimension. They may have trouble sitting through a complete meal or a half-hour television program, and may sleep restlessly.

DYSLEXIA

"Dyslexia" refers to a specific learning disability affecting reading and, nearly always, spelling as well. Dyslexia is a reading disorder associated with neurologic dysfunction rather than other causes, such as emotional problems or lack of opportunity to learn. As such it is characterized by unique patterns of errors in reading and spelling. Most experts now agree that dyslexia may be expressed in various categories or subtypes, and we feel the classifications described by Boder (1973) and Pirozzolo (1979) are most consistent with those encountered in clinical practice. The three subtypes of dyslexia discussed by Boder and Pirozzolo are *dysphonetic* or *auditory-phonetic* dyslexia, *dyseidetic* or *visuo-spatial* dyslexia, and a *mixed type*, which exhibits features of the other two types.

The dyslexic subtype with the highest reported incidence is auditory-phonetic or dysphonetic dyslexia. Such readers have difficulty making subtle discriminations among vowel sounds. They make poor sound-symbol associations, and have difficulty with sound blending and sequencing. In short, the "auditory-phonetic" aspects of reading represent relative weaknesses for such dyslexics, although they tend to have preserved ability to revisualize or recall sight words. Because of this combination of strengths and weaknesses, auditory-phonetic dyslexics have unique spelling patterns, characterized by relatively good ability to spell common words they have encountered frequently, despite extreme difficulty associating letters and sounds to spell less familiar words in a phonetically correct manner.

The second subtype of specific dyslexia, dyseidetic or visuo-spatial dyslexia, is actually the rarest in terms of reported frequency. Studies have reported auditory-phonetic dyslexia in approximately two-thirds of reading disabled children, followed by mixed dyslexia among one-fifth and dyseidetic or visuo-spatial dyslexia in a very small fraction of reading disabled children (Boder & Jarrico, 1982; Telzrow, Century, Redmond, Whitaker, & Zimmerman, 1983). Dyseidetic dyslexics exhibit reading and spelling patterns that are the mirror image of those described for dysphonetic dyslexics. They have difficulty revisualizing words, and may make spelling errors in simple, frequently encountered words. They demonstrate an overreliance on sound-symbol associations, thus exhibiting a tendency to "sound out" even simple words because of difficulty in recalling sight words. Consequently, their spelling is often phonetically correct, though filled with errors. To illustrate, the child with the dyseidetic dyslexic spelling pattern presented at the conclusion of this chapter composed a paragraph about the "Stajue of Libertea."

Mixed dyslexics display reading and spelling weaknesses characteristic of the other two subtypes, and are clearly among the most severely disabled readers. Both reading and spelling skills are often severely impaired, resulting in slow, inconsistent progress in these areas. Mixed dyslexics, especially those who are young, appear to have no usable key to the reading and spelling code; hence, their errors are bizarre and inconsistent (e.g., dictated words followed by spelling attempts may be as follows: half/foxe; forget/tens, etc.).

DYSGRAPHIA

Dysgraphia refers to a neurologic disorder that impairs one's ability to express ideas through writing or written symbols. It frequently occurs in conjunction with dyslexia, although in rare instances individuals may have preserved reading ability despite disordered spelling and handwriting skills (see Case #5). Diagnosis of dysgraphia requires qualitative judgment and consideration of a number of factors, including the youngster's age, intellectual level, and relevant peripheral or central disorders that might impair motor control. For example, a child with spastic cerebral palsy would not be considered specifically dysgraphic, because the spasticity would impair all motor functions and would not be limited to written language performance. Often dysgraphic children enjoy and may excel at other pencil and paper tasks, such as drawing or design copying. The fifth case illustrates a rare type of dysgraphic child whose reading is preserved despite pervasive disorders of spelling and written language.

DYSCALCULIA

The term "dyscalculia" refers to a neurologically based disorder that impairs one's ability to perform mathematical calculations. It is less well understood than reading and spelling disorders, and there is disagreement in the neuropsychological literature about what specific processes may be implicated in dyscalculic disorders.

In our experience, mathematics disorders tend to be displayed as either disorders of computation or reasoning, or both. Children who exhibit disorders of mathematics computation often have extraordinary difficulty memorizing basic arithmetic facts, although when permitted to use a calculator or table of math facts, such children may be able to solve arithmetic problems successfully. Number and letter reversals may be observed, and they may confuse two-digit numbers (e.g., 17 and 71). Multistep arithmetic processes, such as multiplication and long division, are especially difficult. There is some evidence that associates this type of mathematics disorder with weaknesses in perceptual-organizational ability (Rourke & Finlayson, 1978), such that scores on the WISC-R subtests sensitive to these processes (e.g., Picture Completion, Block Design, Object Assembly) may be depressed, and performance on form copying tasks (e.g., Beery, Aphasia Screening Test drawings) may be poor.

Disorders of mathematics reasoning take a quite different form, and are characterized by difficulty in understanding how to apply arithmetic processes, despite mastery of basic mathematics facts. Some experts suggest these weaknesses may be associated with a pervasive language disorder (Rourke & Strang, 1983). We have observed that some children with mathematics reasoning disorders have preserved language skills, although they have a relative weakness in abstract reasoning and concept formation, which might be exhibited by a depressed score on the Reasoning cluster of the Woodcock-Johnson Cognitive Battery or a high error score on the Halstead Category Test.

BACKGROUND INFORMATION
AND PRE-EVALUATION ACTIVITIES

HEALTH HISTORY

Rationale. The importance of a complete medical history in documenting the presence of neuropsychological dysfunction is well recognized in clinical practice. Although this is especially true for children with acute neurologic problems, such as epilepsy, tumors, or head injuries, a thorough medical history also may be contributory when evaluating children without known neurologic involvement who show evidence of neuropsychologically based learning disabilities. Some learning problems may be associated with medical conditions considered benign by the parent, and hence they have not been communicated to school officials. Examples are mild head injuries, intermittent seizure histories, allergies, and treatment with some medications. A systematic medical history may identify these or other circumstances that are of relevance in interpreting test data.

Interview Procedure. It is our experience that parents are most cooperative about communicating information concerning medical, developmental, and family histories if given sufficient time to talk freely; if the interviewer demonstrates genuine interest and sensitivity; and if the purpose for collecting such information in the context of the complete evaluation is explained carefully. We have observed that sometimes it is helpful for the interviewer to be of the same ethnic background as the parent.

It is our practice to combine the health, developmental, and family histories in a discussion with one or both parents. We prefer an interview method that is highly structured for the interviewer and yet permits maximum flexibility for the interviewee. This means that the interviewer must be completely familiar with the types of information desired so that no critical element is omitted, while permitting the parent to determine the sequence in which information is collected. Some parents, for example, may reveal important information about a series of early hospitalizations in the context of describing the birth of the youngster. Following the parent's lead during the interview, we believe, not only provides the most complete information, but also communicates interest and strengthens rapport. For those unfamiliar with this technique, the interview method outlined by Edgar Doll and perpetuated in the revised Vineland Adaptive Behavior Scale (Sparrow, Balla, & Cicchetti, 1984) provides a model for this interview procedure.

Types of information to be collected fall into major categories, such as prenatal history, birth events, neonatal course, disease and illness history, hospitalizations and traumas, past and current medications, and so forth. A model for the categories of information that might be included can be obtained from the Health History Inventory on the System of Multicultural Pluralistic Assessment (SOMPA) (Mercer & Lewis, 1978), a scale with such attractive features as an empirical base and quantitative scoring procedure. However, because this instrument was standardized for use in identifying mentally retarded children and its age range is restrictive, it is not recommended within this context.

During the health history interview, we attempt to discover information that may have been missed in other contexts, such as a routine pediatric physical or educational history. Questions are phrased in general terms to attempt to derive information a parent may not be aware he or she has. For example, when asked to describe the child's eating habits, parents may reveal information about the child's oral motor structure involving biting, chewing, and swallowing; about food preferences and allergies; about self-care skills in feeding; and about parent-child interaction in a sometimes troublesome area. A child who avoids textured foods and whose diet consists largely of pureed or soft dishes may be a candidate for further assessment of oral apraxia or other oral motor involvement. In contrast, a 3-year-old who feeds herself unless her father is home, when she extends the spoon to him and he relents to feed her, is exhibiting behavior probably better explained by a social-interactive rather than a neurologic model.

Within the context of obtaining a good health history are potentially delicate areas that require unusual sensitivity on the part of the interviewer. One example is the prenatal history in cases of maternal drug or alcohol abuse. Although there are instances when parents are too embarrassed or defensive about this information to share it openly, we have found that a quiet, accepting approach, which emphasizes the parent's current concern for the youngster, is most helpful. For example, "Mrs. Jones, it's clear you are very committed to John, and want to help us do whatever we can to identify his learning problems so that he can get the help he needs. One of the things we are learning is that all kinds of experiences pregnant women have can affect the baby, even years later. This includes not only things they eat and drink, but prescription or nonprescription drugs, and whether they're depressed or worried. Think back to when you were pregnant with John, and see if any of these circumstances may have applied."

DEVELOPMENTAL HISTORY

Rationale. Early developmental history can identify general slowness in physical development, which may be an indication of pervasive mental retardation or chronic progressive neuromuscular disorders. In addition, by comparing motor milestones with those that rely on nonmotor cognitive and linguistic processes, it is possible to identify systematic patterns of neuropsychological strengths and weaknesses.

Interview Procedure. We tend to use a limited number of motor and language milestones for which the parent is requested to estimate the age of acquisition. These include sitting alone, crawling, pulling to stand, walking with help, walking alone, alternating feet ascending and descending steps, pedaling a tricycle, and riding a two-wheel bicycle. Nonmotor cognitive and language-related skills for which the parent is asked to provide age estimates include speaking three to four words, vocabulary of 50 words, combining words into three-or-four-word strings, responding to questions regarding function of objects (e.g., "What do we cook on?"), and pre-academic skills relative to a variety of concepts. In addition, because parents' recall often tends to be cloudy and inaccurate, they are asked to give a subjective impression: Was the achievement of these milestones ahead of schedule, within normal limits, or behind schedule? A more comprehensive discussion of comparing language and nonlanguage milestones is included in Chapter 4 of this text and in other works by the authors (Hartlage & Telzrow, 1982a; Telzrow & Hartlage, 1983).

FAMILY AND EDUCATIONAL HISTORY

Rationale. A comprehensive neuropsychological assessment of learning problems should incorporate information about the family history. Such information helps to define incidental learning experiences enjoyed by the child, which may contribute to differentiating between environmental and biological etiology of observable behavior. A child whose single parent has less than a tenth grade education, is unemployed, and has intermittent episodes of depression, will likely have significantly different incidental learning experiences than a child whose parents have college educations and enjoy a stable family environment. Educational level of parent, for example, has repeatedly emerged as a critical predictor of children's success on developmental measures and in school (Hartlage & Telzrow, 1982b; Werner, Honzik, & R. S. Smith, 1968). Collecting information about family history also may provide evidence of familial patterns of chronic learning problems, as noted in many cases of specific learning disabilities (Geschwind & Behan, 1982).

Interview Procedure. A few key questions about family history should be included in the parent interview. Although some of these might be perceived as intrusive and threatening to parents, it is our experience that if adequate respect and concern for the parents are reflected in the interview, they generally respond openly. The first question concerns the handedness of parents, siblings, and the referred child. Handedness is an issue of sometimes debatable consequence, but we generally collect this piece of information in the event it proves useful in the context of other data. It has been reported, for example, that early establishment of a consistent hand preference may be associated with intellectual advantages (A. S. Kaufman, Zalma, & N. L. Kaufman, 1978), particularly in girls (Gottfried & Bathurst, 1983), and that, conversely, delayed establishment may reflect neurologic immaturity or dysfunction. The significance of left-handedness in a child is also of some debate in the literature. However, it is clear that the incidence of left-handedness in populations of disabled children is significantly higher than in the general population (e.g., Tsai, 1982), which has led some to claim that left-handedness in and of itself is a symptom of compromised neurologic integrity (e.g., Bakan, Dibb, & Reed, 1973). In our experience this is likely to be less true if one or certainly both of the child's parents are left-handed, because familial sinistrality suggests the observed phenomenon is an inherited characteristic rather than resultant from an accident at birth. Left-handedness also has been associated with a cluster of other symptoms, including immune diseases (e.g., colitis), migraine, and learning disorders (Geschwind & Behan, 1982). Finally, knowledge about the handedness of the child may be critical to the interpretation of neuropsychological test results, because the lateralization of language and visuo-spatial skills into the left and right hemispheres, respectively, has been shown to be less consistent among left-handed individuals.

A second important piece of information to be included in the family history is the educational level of the parents. As noted above, parent education level is an important correlate of children's performance on educationally related tasks, and is therefore a critical variable in sorting out environmental from biological effects. In our experience, there are two ways this information can be obtained, depending upon the progress of the interview and the perceived reluctance of the parent. The first method is to ask the question in a matter-of-fact manner, at the time other background information is being collected. A second approach, which we tend to use if there is some reluctance evident on the part of the parent early in the interview, is to incorporate this question in the context of a discussion about the child's educational history, as described below.

The third critical area of information to be gleaned from the family history concerns the expression of learning problems among other family members. We generally make such inquiries when discussing the parents' observations about the child's difficulties and what concerns the parent has about the child's learning or school progress. We have found it is extremely helpful to obtain independent home and school reports, because the level and nature of concern may vary across these two settings. We then communicate to the parent in general terms what observations school personnel have made. For example: "Susie's teacher is concerned that she can't work alone; have you observed this at home?" In rare instances, a parent may deny any knowledge of a problem, and may reject any examples of learning difficulty supplied by the interviewer. Much more commonly, a parent will have observed the specific behavior reported (e.g., inability to express ideas in phrases and sentences), but will not have interpreted this as a problem (e.g., "He's just quiet, like me"). In our experience, a posture that accepts the parent's observations while communicating both the specific problem indicators observed and the significance of these, is important to the parent's eventual comprehension and acceptance of the subsequent diagnosis. For example: "It is not typical for 8-year-olds to have as much trouble saying what they want to say as John seems to have. I think this is something we'll want to look at further when we evaluate John."

Within the context of this discussion of the child's difficulties, we seek to identify learning problems in other family members, and, if not ascertained earlier, the educational levels of parents. It is our experience that nearly always parents have made good observations about their children's learning and behavior problems, and are eager to have these listened to by a caring professional. If, in this context, they are asked to recall whether other family members, including themselves, their parents, their siblings, and their other children evidenced any problems with school work, they generally respond without reservation. For example: "Tell me, as you think back to when you and your brothers and sisters went to school, do you recall if any of you had problems in school, either like we've been discussing with Bobby, or perhaps of a different sort? How about Bobby's grandparents - did they ever talk about having any problems in school? Do any of your other children have school-related problems?" Inquiries about educational attainment of the child's parent flow naturally from such discussion. For example: "How much education do you have? And Bobby's father - how much schooling did he complete?"

SUMMARY

A thorough history is an important part of a comprehensive neuropsychological evaluation. We advocate conducting an interview with one or both parents prior to the evaluation of the child. The interview may be conducted in the home, school, or clinic setting, but sufficient time and interviewer experience and empathy are essential in order to obtain the most accurate information. We recommend the use of an interview technique in which the parent is engaged in a discussion about his or her child through broad, general questions followed by specific probes as necessary. Critical elements of the child's medical, developmental, and family history thereby are covered.

Data from the history can assist in structuring the evaluation of the child. If a parent expresses concern about the child's reading skills, but describes the youngster as proficient in math, a different battery of tests is suggested than if the pattern of presenting problems were reversed. Similarly, in cases where the parent describes a family history suggesting genetic disorders (e.g., a Down's syndrome sibling; a cousin with Klinefelter's syndrome), the clinician would be wise to make a special note to examine the child for physical anomalies that may be associated with neurodevelopmental syndromes.

Finally, it is important to emphasize that although a positive medical, developmental, or family history may be of significance, the failure to identify pathognomonic signs in the history should not necessarily be interpreted as an indication of neuropsychological health. The classic maxim, "Absence of evidence is not evidence of absence," illustrates this point succinctly. Though a positive history may encourage and direct the clinician's case investigation, a negative history should not discourage further inquiry.

NEUROPSYCHOLOGICAL TESTING

In conducting direct assessment of the child for suspected learning problems, we employ a model of neuropsychological functioning that incorporates known neuropsychological processes such as language and sensory and motor functions, as well as developmental variability. This concept is critical for pediatric populations. An overview of the model will be presented first, followed by an outline of actual assessment devices and procedures.

MODEL OF NEUROPSYCHOLOGICAL FUNCTIONING

Neuropsychological Processes. Several neuropsychological processes have been identified that are sufficiently discrete and localized that they can be measured by specific instruments or portions of instruments with demonstrated construct validity in relation to these abilities. Language skills, including such component abilities as receptive and expressive language, reading, spelling, and written expression, are one example. Although some of the more complex of these processes (e.g., reading comprehension) rely on the interrelationship of myriad neurologic loci, the foundations of most of these language-related skills can be traced to the integrity of various regions of the left cerebral hemisphere.

Another example of measurable neuropsychological processes are visuo-spatial or perceptual-organization skills. These are observed in the ability to integrate visual details into a meaningful whole and to perceive complex perceptual relationships in objects, and generally have been reported to be lateralized in the right cerebral hemisphere. Impairment in such processes has been observed in difficulty with directionality (e.g., locating one's classroom in a school building, reversal of letters or numbers) and problems with map reading and other visuo-spatial skills. Some evidence suggests that deficits in perceptual-organization ability may be reflected in weaknesses in mathematics (Rourke & Finlayson, 1978).

In addition to the linguistic/visuo-spatial dichotomy, which characterizes the lateral or left-right dimension of brain-behavior relationships, there is the longitudinal or front-back dimension. This dimension is characterized by a motor/sensory dichotomy, reflecting the motor (anterior) and sensory (posterior) regions of the cerebral cortex. The motor strip cuts across both cerebral hemispheres in the frontal lobe, just anterior to the central fissure, a region that controls cortical motor movements of the human body in a point-by-point relationship (Geschwind, 1979). The body is represented on the motor strip in a contralateral, inverted fashion. Thus the uppermost motor functions of the left side of the body (e.g., movement of the tongue) are enervated by the lowest portion of the motor cortex on the right cerebral hemisphere. Impairment of discrete regions of the motor strip therefore would be reflected in motor dysfunction of the corresponding body part. Other, higher cognitive skills subserved by this or contiguous regions may be impaired as well. For example, a common profile observed in dyslexic children includes depressed finger tapping speed on the right hand. Since right-hand finger tapping is interpreted as a measure of left frontal integrity, depressed performance suggests a relative weakness in this region, consistent with the suspected loci for reading disorders (Galaburda, 1983; Galaburda & Kemper, 1979).

The analog to the motor strip in the parietal lobe is the sensory cortex, which is located just posterior to the central fissure. Like the motor cortex, the sensory strip is represented in a contralateral, inverted fashion. The point-by-point relationship here is between the sensory cortex and body parts for sensation or touch. Reduced sensation in specific body parts, such as the hands or legs, may be associated with dysfunction in corresponding regions of the sensory cortex, although other causes, such as peripheral nerve damage or spinal cord injury, must be ruled out. One group of disabled children for whom sensory integrity is especially critical are those who experience cortical blindness as a result of a lesion in the occipital lobe. For some of these children, learning Braille represents an unusual hardship because the vascular disorder or tumor that left the youngster blind also inflicted damage to the sensory regions, impeding the sensitive touch needed to read Braille.

Developmental Variability. The preceding description of measurable neuropsychological processes, although admittedly reduced to a model much simpler than actually reflected in human beings, makes the assessment of neuropsychological abilities appear to be a fairly straightforward process. However, this presumes a static quality to these abilities that does not exist in pediatric populations. Though it is generally true that we can speak of lateralized abilities and the anterior-motor/posterior-sensory dichotomy, the uncharted influence of developmental trends complicates our understanding of how these processes are exhibited in children (e.g., Bolter & Long, 1985). For this reason, neuropsychological assessment of pediatric populations requires clinicians to be familiar with a developmental model in addition to possessing a neuropsychological orientation (Taylor, Fletcher, & Satz, 1984).

A number of developmental models exist that may have relevance for how test data are interpreted, including the theories of Piaget (1975), Vygotsky, and Luria (Flavell, 1977). Key concepts from these theories will be integrated here in presenting a brief developmental model for interpreting the neuropsychological performance of children.

One critical component of any developmental model is that there are qualitative as well as quantitative differences in children at various ages. Hence a 10-year-old does not simply have more of something than his 5-year-old sibling; there is a qualitative difference in their approach to the world and its problems. Theorists have identified broad age groups that seem to characterize qualitatively different categories of processing. In general these seem to be (a) the infant stage: up to age 2 years; (b) the early childhood period: from about age 2 to 6 or 7; (c) the middle childhood period: from ages 6 or 7 to about 11 or 12; and (d) the adolescent period: from about 11 or 12 to late teens. It is interesting to note that the standardization ages of many cognitive batteries seem to correspond to these age clusters (e.g., there are three Wechsler scales, and the K-ABC tasks vary at different ages), and empirically derived neuropsychological batteries, such as the Reitan, prescribe separate measures for younger (ages 5 to 8) and older (ages 9 to 14) children and adults (ages 15 and up). The importance of maintaining a developmental set in the interpretation of test results is illustrated by the case of an 11-year-old not yet capable of reasoning with abstractions and forming hypotheses, skills critical for a good performance on the Category Test. Clinicians must employ knowledge of *both* developmental variability *and* neuropsychological dysfunction in their evaluations of children.

A second premise in our developmental model is that neuromaturation continues throughout the developmental period and hence is reflected in different products and processes at different stages. Luria's (1966) model of neurologic organization is of relevance in this context. Luria described three units of the brain that require increasingly complex neurologic processes. The first unit, relying mainly on subcortical structures, is concerned primarily with arousal, which readies the organism to maintain conditions suitable for survival. Such neurologic processes are most readily observable in the human neonate, whose life work revolves around such crucial functions. Luria's second unit is concerned with reception and integration of sensory information. Within this unit Luria identified primary, secondary, and tertiary areas to describe the increasing complexity of the basic tasks of sensory reception and integration. The primary areas of the second unit, which are built into the structure of the intact central nervous system, are concerned with basic sensory reception of auditory, visual, and tactile information. The secondary areas analyze and integrate this information and, at the tertiary level, interaction and integration across modalities occurs. Progression from the primary to the tertiary areas requires increasing neuromaturation and is evident in a greater degree of hemispheric specialization. The third unit of the brain, as described by Luria, is concerned with output and planning, and tasks comprising such abilities also can be categorized into the increasingly complex processes characteristic of the primary, secondary, and tertiary areas. In unit three, the primary area is concerned with motor output, the secondary area with organization and sequencing of motor acts, and the tertiary area with planning, evaluation, and focusing of attention. The most complex neuropsychological processes in human beings are associated with the tertiary area of unit three and may be compatible with Piaget's stage of formal operations.

Although to some degree Luria's model depicts a developmental hierarchy, there is not a direct and unvarying relationship between the three units of the brain or the primary, secondary, and tertiary areas. As a result, it is not always possible to predict from one stage what the behavioral status will be at another, because an impaired process at an early age might be replaced by intact neurologic functions at a subsequent stage of development, or vice versa. Some neuropsychological processes clearly demonstrate a hierarchy, such that a disruption in early, requisite abilities implies the presence of impairment in related, higher-order skills. Language ability represents a good model for such interdependent skill development, and it is increasingly clear that disruption of early language processes as a result of left hemisphere damage is reflected in atypical language skills at older ages as well (Aram, Ekelman, Rose, & Whitaker, 1985).

However, this hierarchical relationship does not exist exclusively in the neurologic development of children.

Some abilities appear to be subserved by different functional systems at different stages of development, resulting in some discontinuity in performance at various ages. One example of such discontinuity is the issue of subcortical versus cortical control of attention. Some children who exhibit extreme hyperactivity during the preschool years show greater attention and concentration at older ages when control over such abilities is exerted by the tertiary area of unit three of the brain.

Summary. Two major and apparently contradictory principles are implied by this model of neuropsychological functioning. One is that certain neuropsychological skills are sufficiently discrete and localized to be identified and measured in children. The second is that children, by their very nature, introduce the variable of inconstancy, which is reflected in discontinuity across the developmental period. When considered together, these two characteristics of the neuropsychological development of children suggest that although some conclusions can be made in some areas about the neuropsychological integrity of children, the degree to which it is possible to make precise diagnostic and prognostic statements is less than for adults.

HYPOTHESIS TESTING

Hypothesis testing is a mainstay of neuropsychological assessment, and can be employed successfully with children. A clinician who is knowledgeable about both neuropsychological functioning and developmental variability can integrate findings from diverse data sources to develop hypotheses regarding the nature, type, and, if indicated, locus or loci of dysfunction observed in a particular child.

Figures 1 and 2 illustrate how test results might be correlated in a model of sequential hypothesis generation. The two examples represent contrasting patterns of neuropsychological strengths and weaknesses. Figure 1 depicts a situation where developmental language milestones are consistently slower than nonlanguage milestones, measures of verbal IQ are consistently lower than measures of nonverbal IQ, and the receptive language scaled score is considerably lower than constructional praxis scaled scores. In addition, the youngster's right-hand performance is poorer (i.e., more

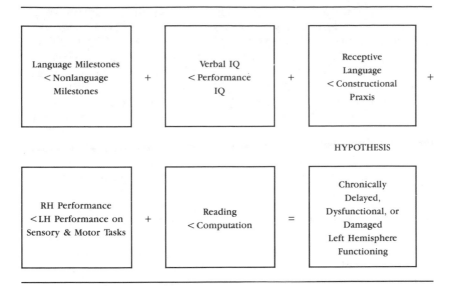

Figure 1. Hypothesis Testing - Situation 1

depressed from expectancy levels) than left-hand performance on motor and sensory functions, and academic skill levels on reading have lower standard scores than those for calculation on tests such as the Wide

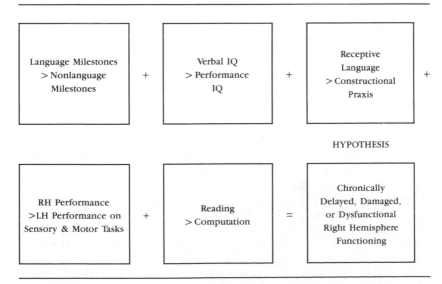

Figure 2. Hypothesis Testing - Situation 2

Range Achievement Test (WRAT). Such a composite is consistent with a hypothesis of chronically delayed, dysfunctional, or damaged left hemisphere functioning. Figure 2 portrays the reversed pattern of data, which is compatible with a hypothesis of chronically delayed, dysfunctional, or damaged right hemisphere functioning.

In addition to generating hypotheses about the loci of dysfunction and associated patterns of strengths and weaknesses, as illustrated by Figures 1 and 2, it also may be possible to infer etiology from the available data. Figures 3, 4, and 5 illustrate the manner in which various patterns of historical information and test results suggest differing etiologies.

When developmental milestones indicate consistently higher levels than are reflected on psychometric, academic, and other performance measures of current function, and there are no compelling data to support the presence of functional (e.g., schizophrenia), social (e.g., child abuse, divorce), or other (e.g., drug abuse) factors, it may be hypothesized that some acquired insult to the central nervous system may be etiologic in this discrepancy (Figure 3). Greater specificity may be

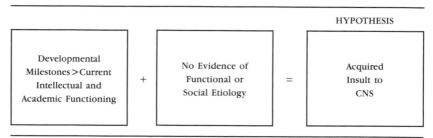

Figure 3. Hypothesis Testing - Situation 3

possible when the current levels of function show apparent diffuse, generalized dysfunction, even though some abilities, such as those involving receptive language or word recognition, may be comparatively intact with respect to developmental history. In this instance, it may be hypothesized that observed deficits are associated with generalized insult to the central nervous system, which might be caused by infectious, degenerative, anoxic, or toxic factors (Figure 4). When medical data concerning such possible factors are available, further questioning and evaluation to relate such phenomena as time of onset relative to changes in performance levels is appropriate. If the child has not had a medical evaluation, referral

HYPOTHESIS

| Neuropsychological Test Data Reveal Diffuse Generalized Dysfunction | ± | Discrete Abilities Intact on Developmental History | = | Generalized CNS Insult (e.g., Infection, Anoxic, or Toxic Effects) |

Figure 4. Hypothesis Testing - Situation 4

may be helpful for identifying possible treatment or continuity care indications.

Figure 5 illustrates a situation where current levels of function show multifocal but not diffuse patterns of impairment, and there is evidence (e.g., from parental and teacher reports) of behavior changes. Several possible etiologies are suggested by such a composite. Additional investigation should first involve questions concerning possible head trauma. If noncontributory, further evaluation concerning possible cerebral blood flow interruptions of given vessels that might relate to patterns of impairment noted on testing should be undertaken. Given this consideration, more detailed family history relative to possible circulatory problems such as aneurisms may be helpful. If these data are noncontributory, further evaluation concerning possible neoplastic (tumor)

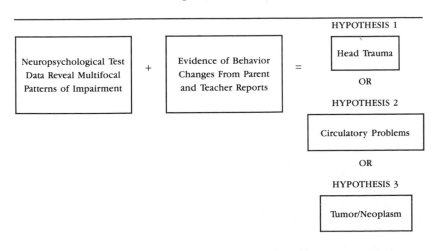

Figure 5. Hypothesis Testing - Situation 5

involvement may be appropriate. Although the latter two considerations are considerably less common as etiologic bases of problems in children than traumatic head injuries, these conditions obviously indicate prompt referral to appropriate neurologic specialists. Neuropsychological assessment of such conditions requires considerable skill and sophistication, and generally should not be undertaken by psychologists with limited training and experience in neuropsychology.

MEASURABLE ABILITIES
AND APPROPRIATE INSTRUMENTS

Cognitive Ability.   There are two major objectives in the assessment of cognitive ability. The first of these is to determine the overall level of intellectual ability in order to establish an anchor point for other skills and to predict academic achievement levels. A second goal of intellectual assessment is to identify unique patterns of performance that might suggest intra-individual strengths and weaknesses in neuropsychological abilities.

The first objective is fairly straightforward, and relies on normative assessment. Any of the measures of intellectual ability listed in Table 1 (pp. 46-47) may be appropriate for this purpose, provided there are no unique student characteristics (e.g., certain handicapping conditions) that rule out the selection of a particular instrument.

The second goal of intellectual assessment - the identification of neuropsychological strengths and weaknesses - is somewhat more complex. Our approach to this problem derives from research that suggests a two-factor model of cognitive processing. These two styles of information processing have been given a variety of names such as left hemisphere and right hemisphere, sequential and simultaneous, and linguistic and visuo-spatial. Although the names assigned these factors vary, we have found that the processing abilities identified by independent researchers share much in common; that there appear to be two, fairly discrete ways of processing information that might be described as verbal, sequential, analytic, and linguistic, as opposed to holistic, visuo-spatial, and simultaneous.   Furthermore, though all persons are capable of employing both means of processing, there is evidence suggesting that many individuals have a preferred style of information processing (Levy, 1985) that may be biologically based (Geschwind, 1979; Geschwind & Levitsky, 1968).

Working from the premise that there are two styles of information processing, and that some children, particularly those with learning problems, may evidence unique disparity between the two processing strategies, we attempt to identify specific patterns in such abilities by analyzing the individual's performance on various cognitive measures. Scales we favor for conducting such analyses are the Wechsler Scales (WPPSI, WISC-R, and WAIS-R), the Kaufman Assessment Battery for Children (K-ABC), and the Cognitive Scale of the Woodcock-Johnson Psychoeducational Battery (WJPB).

Wechsler Scales. The first and most straightforward test of intra-individual variability on the Wechsler scales derives from a comparison of Wechsler's two-factor (i.e., Verbal-Performance) solution. In determining whether Verbal-Performance differences are significant, clinicians are reminded that two tests of observed differences are necessary. The first is the test of *statistical* significance, which defines the probability that the observed V-P difference could occur by chance alone. The second, and perhaps more meaningful test, describes the expression of this V-P difference in the standardization population. The value of conducting both tests is illustrated by the case of a V-P difference of 15 points on the WISC-R. Although such a difference is statistically significant (i.e., would be unlikely to occur by chance alone), it is fairly common, occurring in approximately 20% of the standardization population. Tables specifying levels of statistical significance and percent occurrence in the standardization population can be found in Sattler (1982, p. 572).

A second procedure for analyzing Wechsler scores examines intra-individual variability in subtest performance. This procedure includes an analysis of the range of subtest scores, computation of the student's mean score, and the identification of significant strengths and weaknesses that fall approximately one standard deviation either side of this mean. Precise directions for conducting such subtest analyses have been described by A. S. Kaufman (1979) and Sattler (1982). The *average* youngster in the WISC-R standardization sample demonstrates a range of 7 scaled score points, and a range

TABLE 1: COMMON INSTRUMENTS USED IN ASSESSMENT OF SUSPECTED LEARNING PROBLEMS IN SCHOOL-AGED CHILDREN

Assessment Category	Instruments	Publisher
Cognitive Ability	1. Wechsler Intelligence Scale for Children (WISC-R)	The Psychological Corporation
	2. Kaufman Assessment Battery for Children (K-ABC)	American Guidance Services
	3. Stanford-Binet Intelligence Scale	Riverside Publishing Company
	4. Leiter International Performance Scale	Stoelting Publishing Company
	5. Woodcock-Johnson Psychoeducational Battery (WJPB) - Cognitive Scale	DLM-Teaching Resources
Basic Language Skills (Listening & Speaking)	1. Test of Language Development - Primary (TOLD-P)	PRO-ED
	2. Test of Language Development - Intermediate (TOLD-I)	PRO-ED
	3. Test of Adolescent Language (TOAL)	PRO-ED
	4. Clinical Evaluation of Language Functions (CELF)	Charles Merrill
	5. Token Test for Children	DLM-Teaching Resources
	6. Aphasia Screening Test	Neuropsychology Press
	7. Diagnostic Achievement Battery (DAB)	PRO-ED
Reading	1. Woodcock Test of Reading Mastery	American Guidance Services
	2. Woodcock-Johnson Psychoeducational Battery (WJPB) - Achievement Scale	DLM-Teaching Resources
	3. K-ABC Achievement Scale	American Guidance Services
	4. Diagnostic Reading Scales (Spache)	CTB/McGraw-Hill
	5. Diagnostic Achievement Battery (DAB)	PRO-ED
	6. Boder Test of Reading-Spelling Patterns	Grune & Stratton, Inc.
Written Expression	1. Woodcock-Johnson Psychoeducational Battery (WJPB) - Achievement Scale	DLM-Teaching Resources

Assessment Category	Instruments	Publisher
Written Expression (Continued)	2. Test of Written Language (TOWL) 3. Test of Adolescent Language (TOAL) 4. Aphasia Screening Test 5. Diagnostic Achievement Battery (DAB)	PRO-ED PRO-ED Neuropsychology Press PRO-ED
Mathematics	1. K-ABC Achievement Battery 2. Woodcock-Johnson Psychoeducational Battery (WJPB) - Achievement Scale 3. Key Math Test	American Guidance Services DLM-Teaching Resources American Guidance Services
Motor/Visual Motor Ability	1. Finger Oscillation 2. Grip Strength 3. Physical Dexterity Tasks - System of Multi-cultural, Pluralistic Assessment (SOMPA) 4. Aphasia Screening Test 5. Developmental Test of Visual Motor Integration (Beery VMI)	Reitan Neuropsychological Laboratory Reitan Neuropsychological Laboratory The Psychological Corporation Neuropsychology Press Follett Publishing Company
Sensory Ability	1. Sensory-Perceptual Tasks (e.g., finger localization, fingertip number writing, hand face test) 2. Motor Free Visual Perception Test	See Benton, Hamsher, Varney, and Spreen, 1983; Reitan, 1979 Academic Therapy Publications
Social Behavior	1. Connors Behavior Rating Scale 2. Child Behavior Checklist 3. Devereux Elementary School Behavior Rating Scale	See Connors, 1969, 1982 University Associates in Psychiatry The Devereux Foundation
Other Measures of Neuro-psychological Ability	1. Trail Making Test 2. Halstead Category Test	Reitan Neuropsychological Laboratory Reitan Neuropsychological Laboratory

of 9 points (e.g., 5 to 14) is still considered within normal limits (A. S. Kaufman, 1979). It is important to note how this contradicts the well-accepted myth that subtest scatter is pathognomonic of a learning disability.

Within this discussion of analyzing subtest variability for patterns of neuropsychological dysfunction, we need to consider the Selz-Reitan scatter index. The Selz-Reitan index is a procedure for quantifying subtest variability on the WISC-R (high subtest minus low subtest divided by subtest mean). The guidelines outlined by Selz and Reitan (1979) indicate that a scatter index of 1.0 or greater suggests possible neuropsychological dysfunction, with indices in the range of 1.4 to 1.78 associated with probable neurologic impairment, and indices exceeding this figure indicating definite neuropsychological dysfunction. As Gutkin and Reynolds (1981) point out, two important variables influence the scatter index. The first, obviously, is IQ level, with lower IQ values resulting in considerably higher scatter index scores. Gutkin and Reynolds also have reported that race is a potent variable in interpreting the Selz-Reitan index, because a higher percentage of black students in the WISC-R standardization sample have "significant" scatter index scores than whites at all IQ levels. To illustrate, a Selz-Reitan index of 1.3, considered to be indicative of possible neurologic impairment by Selz and Reitan, occurs in approximately 15% of black children with IQs in the average range, but only in approximately 9% of white students within this ability level. Readers are encouraged to consider the findings of Gutkin and Reynolds (1981), as well as those of Coolidge, Bracken, Andrews, and Pennington (1985) when interpreting the Selz-Reitan scatter index scores.

Another procedure we favor for analyzing the presence of intra-individual variability on the WISC-R utilizes a procedure outlined by Bannatyne (1974) for recategorizing subtest scores. The Bannatyne procedure identifies four cognitive factors that can be derived by clustering subtest scores as described below. The *acquired knowledge* factor is composed of subtests Information, Arithmetic, and Vocabulary. The *sequential* factor comprises subtests Arithmetic, Digit Span, and Coding. The three subtests Similarities, Vocabulary, and Comprehension define the *verbal conceptualization* factor, and finally, the *spatial* factor is composed of subtests Picture Completion, Block Design, and Object Assembly.

Individual factor scores are derived by obtaining an average score for the subtests comprising that factor.

Bannatyne's early work suggested that the pattern of factor scores for learning disabled children favored spatial ability, with other scores, in descending order, being verbal conceptualization, sequential, and acquired knowledge. Some data have supported the existence of a "spatially competent LD child" (Bannatyne, 1978; Rugel, 1974; Zingale & M. D. Smith, 1978), though others have disputed these findings (Henry & Wittman, 1981). We now realize that there are subtypes of learning disabled children, and although the spatial > sequential pattern is fairly common among reading disabled children, other profiles may be identified as well (A. S. Kaufman, 1981). We have found recategorization of the WISC-R scores according to Bannatyne's model helpful in identifying patterns of cognitive strengths and weaknesses (e.g., Telzrow et al., 1983). The case studies included at the end of this chapter illustrate this and other analyses derived from the Wechsler scales.

Kaufman Assessment Battery for Children. The K-ABC is a relatively recent measure of intellectual ability and was derived from the two-factor model of cognitive processing outlined above. Separate scores are reported for Sequential and Simultaneous ability, as well as a total score, or Mental Processing Composite (MPC). In our experience there are advantages and disadvantages to the K-ABC; despite its usefulness in some cases, it is difficult to predict those for which it will provide new information.

The excellent manuals that accompany the K-ABC provide detailed instructions for conducting intra-individual comparisons. These follow the same basic procedures outlined above for the Wechsler scales. The K-ABC manuals also include tables that facilitate comparison of the Sequential with the Simultaneous scales and help in determining significant strengths and weaknesses among subtest scores. The second and third case studies at the conclusion of this chapter illustrate interpretation of the K-ABC with other neuropsychological test data.

Woodcock-Johnson Psychoeducational Battery (WJPB) Cognitive Scale. Although the achievement portion of this battery is more widely used in educational settings, we recommend the cognitive scale because of the cognitive factors that can be derived. It is important to note that the WJPB should not be interpreted as an intelligence test in the same way as the Binet, Wechsler scales, and K-ABC are used (Hessler, 1982). Total score differences of from one-half to one standard deviation between the WJPB and the WISC-R have been reported (Reeve, Hall, & Zakreski, 1979; Ysseldyke, Shinn, & Epps, 1981), and in our experience the WJPB broad cognitive ability score for a given individual is likely to be significantly lower than scores on these other tests. Nevertheless, comparison of the cognitive factor scores on the WJPB can provide useful information about a youngster's neuropsychological processing strategies.

The WJPB cognitive scale has four cognitive cluster scores: Verbal Ability, Reasoning, Visual-Perceptual Speed, and Memory. The last three, in particular, are not as clearly available from other cognitive measures, and hence the WJPB scores can provide useful information. Research using the WJPB has described three major profiles of scores on the battery. The first subtype is exemplified by a depressed Verbal score, together with preserved Reasoning abilities. This profile is commonly observed in children who have reading and spelling problems. The second profile is essentially an inverse of the first, and is characterized by a high Verbal score together with a depressed Reasoning factor. This pattern of scores often is observed in children with arithmetic problems. A third, less common subtype demonstrates weaknesses in Memory and Visual-Perceptual Speed, a pattern that suggests some attention deficits or some difficulties in speeded perceptual motor performance (Hessler, 1982).

In interpreting the WJPB, two cautions are in order. First, two of the cognitive factors - Verbal Ability and Reasoning - utilize a suppressor variable in deriving cluster scores. Although the assumption is that the statistical influence of the suppressor operates in expected fashion for most students, clinicians must examine the relationship of the main subtests to the suppressor variable in these two factors to make certain the cluster score reflects the ability in an accurate rather than an artifactual fashion. Second, the Memory cluster, though sensitive, assesses only a limited component of memory via two auditory short-term memory tasks. One of these, in particular (Numbers Reversed), may be especially vulnerable to the effects of attention deficits. Weaknesses in this cluster may need to be explored further to ascertain the precise weaknesses in neuropsychological abilities tapped by this factor.

Basic Language Skills (Listening and Speaking). Oral expression and listening comprehension are fundamental language skills affected by neuropsychological dysfunction. The grossest disorders are likely to be reflected by significant deficits on cognitive measures, but more subtle problems may be identified through careful assessment of speaking and listening.

A number of standardized tests, such as those listed in Table 1, are appropriate for the evaluation of either or both of these component skills. Because of difficulties that arise when comparing scores from two separate measures using different standardization samples, instruments that report both receptive and expressive language scores (e.g., CELF, TOLD, TOAL) are especially useful. The Aphasia Screening Test, part of the Halstead-Reitan Neuropsychological Test Battery, is useful in identifying some unusual language disorders such as dysnomia and auditory-verbal agnosia. However, because interpretation calls for a pathognomonic sign approach requiring considerable clinical experience, it is not widely used in educational settings.

Reading. The assessment of reading ability, like cognitive assessment, requires that both the level and pattern of performance be established. The level of reading ability, both word recognition and reading comprehension, can be determined by a variety of the norm-referenced measures included in Table 1. The procedure used to establish reading comprehension levels varies somewhat from test to test. For example, the Woodcock-Johnson and Woodcock Reading Mastery Tests use a silent cloze procedure (in which the student fills in a word missing from a passage), whereas the K-ABC uses a gestural response following silent reading. Because the assessment method may influence performance (e.g., a youngster with ideomotor apraxia may have difficulty responding to the K-ABC Reading/Understanding task for reasons unrelated to his reading ability), such factors should be considered in test selection.

A qualitative assessment of reading patterns is recommended as part of a thorough neuropsychological evaluation because of research that suggests reading disorders may be expressed differently in various youngsters. The Boder Test of Reading-Spelling Patterns is helpful in this regard (Boder & Jarrico, 1982). Although the Boder Test has received some criticism because of its unorthodox psychometric properties (Reynolds, 1984), nevertheless it has been recognized as a useful clinical tool (Nockleby & Galbraith, 1984; Telzrow et al., 1983). The Boder test utilizes reading and spelling patterns as the basic elements for identifying the presence and type of neurologically based reading disorders. In general Boder and Jarrico identify as "dysphonetic" those readers who have moderately poor word recognition skills and whose spelling of common words is superior to their ability to associate sounds and symbols in producing "good phonic equivalents" (GFEs). "Dyseidetic" readers have moderately poor word recognition skills; they are better able to spell even difficult words phonetically correctly than to revisualize and spell correctly common words that are phonetically irregular. The "mixed" dyslexic reader demonstrates spelling weaknesses in both visuo-spatial and auditory-phonetic areas and exhibits extremely poor word recognition skills. Case studies #2, #3, and #4 demonstrate the reading and spelling patterns of the three types of dyslexic readers.

Written Expression. In our experience there are two major neuropsychological disorders that affect written language skills. The first and probably most common neuropsychological basis of written language disorders is a pervasive weakness in general language ability. Individuals with such disorders have difficulties with listening and speaking, and thus we can predict that they will have difficulty in the higher language skills inherent in written discourse as well. A second neuropsychological disorder associated with deficits in written expression is dysgraphia, a fairly rare syndrome resulting in unique difficulty in expressing ideas in written symbols. The handwriting of such individuals is unusually poor, with frequent directional problems and a tendency to write over and over letters. Many dysgraphic children continue to print rather than use cursive writing on into adolescence, and even their manuscript printing resembles that of a second or third grader. Their spelling is often extremely poor as well, and the unique difficulty presented by these mechanical weaknesses makes any sort of composition a monumental task. Such children may nevertheless have good basic language skills and may be able to dictate creative, well-organized passages.

Neuropsychological assessment of written expression abilities requires the evaluation of mechanical skills such as handwriting, punctuation, and spelling, as well as higher level language abilities relating to syntax, grammar, and composition. The norm-referenced measures listed in Table 1 do an adequate job of assessing many of the mechanical skills noted above, although the Woodcock-Johnson written language cluster does not require composition of a passage, thus precluding appraisal of handwriting and composition skills. Assessment of dysgraphia, in particular, requires clinical judgment derived from considerable experience with written language skills of children at various ages. The Test of Written Language (TOWL), the TOAL, and the Diagnostic Achievement Battery (DAB) all include extensive samples of written language ability, although we have found that the scores derived from the former two instruments may result in an unusual number of false negative (TOWL) and false positive (TOAL) errors.

Mathematics. The assessment of arithmetic ability in children requires an evaluation of computation and mathematics reasoning. The normative measures outlined in Table 1 assess both these elements, although separate scores for computation and reasoning may not be reported. The Woodcock-Johnson Achievement Scale reports a single mathematics cluster score. It is possible to plot the raw scores for the two subtests comprising the cluster score (Computation and Applied Problems) on the back of the WJPB protocol form to determine whether or not there are significant differences between these two subtests. If so, separate scores for the two subtests should be computed, using Marston and Ysseldyke (1980), because the single cluster score is likely to overestimate one skill and underestimate the other.

The Arithmetic subtest score on the K-ABC incorporates both computation and mathematical reasoning tasks. An item analysis of the individual's performance can be conducted to determine whether or not a pattern of computation strengths and reasoning weaknesses, or vice versa, is suggested. The two case studies in the fourth chapter illustrate how such an item analysis can provide important diagnostic information for preschool children.

Motor Ability. Assessment of the child's motor ability is an important means of evaluating overall central nervous system integrity at both subcortical and cortical levels, as well as identifying left-right asymmetries that are neuropsychologically relevant. Assessment of motor function begins during the pre-evaluation parent interview, with questions regarding early developmental milestones and the current status of self-help and recreational activities. Children whose motor milestones appear to have been delayed, who continue to have difficulty with activities of daily living that require complex motor movements (e.g., cutting meat with a knife), and who prefer sedentary to active pastimes, may exhibit mild to moderate motor dysfunction. Direct appraisal of motor ability begins at initial contact with the child. We use these early "getting acquainted" moments to create situations that require clinically relevant responses, including motor movements. Through careful observation of how the child sits down and rises from a chair, removes and hangs up a coat, walks, manipulates objects and uses a pencil, and whether or not drooling is evident, we can begin to establish some hypotheses about motor ability. In younger children or those for whom there is some special question about motor development, we might arrange to have a meal or snack with the child or to observe the child on the playground or in the gym or therapy room.

More formal assessment of motor ability can be conducted using any or all of the measures listed in Table 1. The SOMPA Physical Dexterity Tasks are standardized for children aged 5 to 12. They are especially useful for clinicians who have not yet developed a sense of typical versus atypical motor responses at various ages because the directions for administering and scoring the tasks are quite explicit. Performance that is deemed to be "at risk" on one or more of the subtests of the SOMPA tasks may suggest immature or impaired development of the central nervous system, which might be explored further with additional testing.

The finger oscillation task is included in many neuropsychological batteries (e.g., Knights & Norwood, undated; Reitan, 1979). This task is designed to identify depressed level of performance that may indicate diffuse anterior dysfunction of the cerebral cortex (because of the locus of the motor strip, in the frontal region, as described above). Other possible reasons for decreased finger tapping speed on one or both hands include subcortical dysfunction and peripheral involvement. These causes should be explored further during the history and direct assessment of the child. In addition to overall level of performance, a comparison of left- and right-hand finger tapping may reveal decreased motor integrity on one side of the body, suggesting the possibility of contralateral brain dysfunction.

Administration procedures for the finger tapping task vary slightly from one battery to another. Reitan's (1979) procedure calls for reaching criterion (five consecutive trials within a range of five taps) on the preferred hand before going to the nonpreferred hand. Three trials are administered, one immediately following another, followed by a brief rest period of 1 to 2 minutes, and an additional two trials or more if necessary until the criterion is reached. The norms for older children (ages 9 to 14) were based on the use of the manual finger tapper. The procedure described by Knights and Norwood (undated) varies somewhat (e.g., the hands alternate from trial to trial), and norms given are based on use of the electric tapper (Knights & Norwood, 1980).

We generally use the manual finger tapper available from Reitan's laboratory and follow his administration procedures. We also favor norms reported by Boll and Reitan (1972) and Knights and Moule (1968). A typical finger tapping pattern usually reflects a 10% faster tapping speed on the preferred hand. Performance that varies from this - more than a 10% difference between the two hands, approximately the same tapping speed for the two hands, or the nonpreferred hand faster - may suggest the presence of an atypical neuropsychological pattern. Several of the case studies reported at the end of this chapter demonstrate clinically significant finger tapping patterns.

For evaluation of upper extremity motor strength, a grip dynamometer provides an objective measure with extensive normative data for children of various ages. Generally unrelated to intellectual ability, this measure provides for a comparison of an individual's motor strength with age and sex expectancies as well as the left and right sides of the body. Although not specifically diagnostic of underlying neuropsychological pathology or dysfunction, a measure of grip strength can clarify questions concerning recency versus chronicity of problems, especially in conjunction with developmental history and other measures such as rate of rapid finger oscillation. Comparatively depressed right-hand grip strength may indicate chronic dysfunction of anterior portions of the left cerebral hemisphere in a child also displaying delayed expressive language milestones, poor performance on measures of expressive language, and depressed right-hand rate of rapid finger oscillation. Conversely, in a child with good language developmental milestones and adequate performance on psychometric language measures, good right-hand grip strength combined with impaired rate of right-hand rapid finger oscillation may suggest a more recent onset of left hemisphere motor dysfunction. Muscle strength may not yet reflect disuse atrophy, whereas the comparatively more sensitive rate of rapid finger oscillation depression on the right hand may be a sign of recent onset. Occasionally, rate of rapid finger oscillation could be depressed by cerebellar dysfunction, while grip strength, comparatively independent of cerebellar involvement, could be intact. This is more likely to occur in children treated with anticonvulsant medication that has cerebellar toxicity as a side effect. Because a number of non-neuropsychological phenomena are associated with asymmetries on this measure, one must be careful not to overinterpret such a pattern. A child engaged in a unilateral focused sport such as tennis may develop above average grip strength in the preferred hand through exercise. When grip asymmetry is the only striking finding, further questioning or other evaluation may be appropriate.

The drawing tasks (Aphasia Screening Test drawings and the Developmental Test of Visual Motor Integration) listed in Table 1 are not pure measures of motor integrity, but nevertheless they may be sensitive to specific and generalized neuropsychological impairment. Drawing tasks, especially in young children, tend to be a good reflection of general developmental level (Beery, 1982; Gesell et al., 1940). Rather definitive age expectations have been identified for copying simple geometric shapes, such as circle (age 3), square (age 4), triangle (age 5), Greek cross (age 6), and diamond (age 7). Drawing deficiencies in the presence of other indicators of average intellectual ability may suggest either specific motor deficiencies or constructional dyspraxia that may be associated with right hemisphere dysfunction. The opposite pattern - age appropriate drawings and subnormal IQ - may suggest the presence of language-related neuropsychological deficits resulting in a depressed IQ score. It also should be noted that because figure drawing (both of human and geometric figures) is so strongly developmentally linked, children with moderate to severe levels of mental retardation would be expected to demonstrate similar delays in their drawing. Such a pattern probably reflects a generalized cognitive delay rather than a specific right lateralized or anterior dysfunction.

When a child reproduces a design in an unsatisfactory way, and such factors as general mental ability do not seem to be viable explanations, it may be possible to separate perceptual from motor and executory problems by simple inquiry. After the test is completed, for example, the examiner might say, "Now I want to show you some designs, and you tell me whether the ones you drew are the same or different from the ones I show you." If the child misrepresented the design but says that it is the same as the stimulus design, perceptual factors may be involved. If, conversely, the child reports the designs are different and on a second attempt still misproduces the design and again recognizes the difference, motor-executory factors may be causative. The nature of the difficulty can now be delineated more precisely. Taken in conjunction with other motor-dependent tasks, such as many of the Wechsler subtests, hypotheses about the integrity of the child's cortical motor functioning can be advanced.

Sensory Ability. Assessment of the child's sensory abilities can identify central or peripheral impairments to vision, hearing, and touch that may be associated with learning problems. Vision and hearing screenings are considered routine parts of a comprehensive neuropsychological assessment, with subsequent referral to appropriate specialists when indicated. Sensory-perceptual tasks such as fingertip number writing, finger localization, and the hand-face test are means of assessing the integrity of the child's sensory system, as well as identifying any left-right asymmetries of a more posterior locus.

In the fingertip number writing task, four numbers are written on the fingertips of both hands, producing a total of 20 such stimuli to each hand. In the case of a younger child who has not yet been taught numbers, or an older child of limited mental ability who has not yet learned numbers sufficiently well to recognize them, symbols such as X and O can be substituted. First the numbers (or symbols) are written on the palm of the hand to insure that the child can identify them. To help minimize possible effects of boredom or fatigue (or such occasional phenomena as clusters of absence seizures), numbers can be written alternatively on all fingers of first one hand and then the other (e.g., R-L, R-L, R-L, R-L), until each hand has received four sequences of one number written on each fingertip. Numbers (or symbols) can be traced using a dry ball-point pen, a mechanical pencil without lead, or a metal stylus or similar device.

Normative expectancy levels for performance on this task are available for children of different ages, and can be used to assess levels of performance on this ability relative to other levels of function such as global mental ability (e.g., Finlayson & Reitan, 1976). Because performance on this sort of task can be influenced by non-neuropsychological phenomena such as injury to given cervical nerves, the distribution of fingers on which difficulty in recognition is observed should be noted. The little and ring fingers, middle and index fingers, and thumb, having different cervical enervation (C8, C7, and C6, respectively), occasionally may reflect clusters of misperceptions related to cervical rather than central nervous system impairment. Thus a pattern of errors on one (or both) hands that is confined to numbers written on the ring and little fingers may represent a C8 dysfunction rather than central nervous system processing difficulty. With this in mind, consistent failure to recognize numbers written on fingers with a single cervical distribution, while recognizing numbers written on all other fingers of the hand, may indicate possible peripheral injury, or require further testing to help minimize false positive identification of parietal dysfunction. With respect to false positive errors, dysfunction of the parietal lobe of the dominant hemisphere occasionally can produce bilateral astereognostic errors. In general, however, the recognition of numbers (or symbols) written on fingertips represents a good screening procedure for function of the sensory strip contralateral to the hand being stimulated. Besides being a useful procedure for evaluation of this function, it is also fairly uninfluenced by environmental or cultural factors. Detailed descriptions of the administrative procedures and normative data for the fingertip number writing task, as well as other measures of sensory-perceptual abilities, are provided by Reitan (1979); Benton, Hamsher, Varney, and Spreen (1983); and Knights and Norwood (undated, 1980).

Social Behavior. The neuropsychological aspects of social behavior are receiving increasing attention (e.g., Dorman, 1982; Golden & Sawicki, 1985). For this reason, we generally include a quantitative measure of social behavior in a neuropsychological assessment of learning problems. The data collected via a teacher or parent behavior rating scale (or, ideally, both) can be interpreted within the context of other neuropsychological findings to describe social behavior of presumed neuropsychological origin. Table 1 lists scales that we use for this purpose.

Other Measures. We often include two specialized neuropsychological tasks as part of an assessment of suspected learning problems. Although these are not linked to discrete brain regions or specific neuropsychological abilities such as language or motor skills, the two tests included in Table 1 nevertheless are sensitive to neurologic dysfunction in children (Reitan, 1971; Selz, 1981; Selz & Reitan, 1979).

The Trail Making Test requires the child to connect circled numbers (Trails A) and letters and numbers (Trails B) in rapid sequence. Children with neurological deficits show significantly slower performance times on both Parts A and B than do their normal peers. Although a poor performance on the Trail Making Test does not have localizing significance or aid in identification of educationally relevant strengths and weaknesses, it nevertheless can help to document neurologic etiology for other observed deficits.

The Halstead Category Test is a measure of higher order reasoning and concept formation. The original version (described in Reitan, 1979) requires an expensive, cumbersome apparatus, although revisions have utilized a computer adaptation and a booklet form (DeFilippis & McCampbell, 1979). Despite the obvious advantages of these revised forms, their validity with children has not been demonstrated, and Reitan and his associates do not equate these revisions with the original device.

In our experience the Category Test is an excellent supplement to the assessment of children with learning problems. A high error score on this task frequently is observed in children who have deficits in mathematics reasoning. A poor Category Test score also may be associated with poor attention and concentration, immature behavior, failure to monitor one's own actions, and poor social judgment - all behavioral characteristics that have been associated with frontal lobe dysfunction (e.g., Malloy, Webster, & Russell, 1985; McKay et al., 1985). Such children may ask direct, embarrassing questions of others and engage in socially inappropriate actions. A depressed score on the Category Test also can occur in bright children who nevertheless have difficulty reasoning in an abstract fashion and therefore may experience school difficulties in advanced subject areas.

Summary. A comprehensive assessment of suspected learning problems in school-aged children should sample a variety of neuropsychological abilities. These include general cognitive ability (using a measure that permits analysis of information processing patterns) and the range of educationally relevant abilities such as basic language skills, reading, written language, and mathematics. Specialized neuropsychological tasks sensitive to left-right motor or sensory asymmetries or generalized neurologic dysfunction complete the comprehensive assessment of learning problems and help to establish viable intervention programs.

INTERVENTION WITH
LEARNING DISABLED CHILDREN

Historically, the focus of clinical practice in neuropsychology has been on diagnosis of brain impairment. More recently, due to the dual effects of improved neurologic diagnostic techniques (e.g., CT scan, positron emission tomography [PET scan], brain electrical activity mapping [BEAM], magnetic resonance imaging [MRI]) and the implications which can be derived from neuropsychological assessment, increasing effort is being directed toward the rehabilitation of brain-injured individuals (Dean, 1982, 1986). Neuropsychologically based interventions are particularly applicable to educational settings (Gaddes, 1983; Hartlage & Telzrow, 1985) despite infrequent use in this context. The remainder of this chapter describes a model of educational intervention derived from neuropsychological principles and illustrates how this approach might be applied to populations of learning disabled children.

BASIC PRINCIPLES OF INTERVENTION

Three basic models of educational intervention have been described in the literature (Cronbach & Snow, 1977). The first model is called a *remediation of deficits* approach, in which a skill deficit is identified and direct instruction is used to teach the missing skill. For example, if a student could not identify 50 words from the Dolch word list (a list of 500 commonly encountered words used in early reading instruction) on flash cards, a remediation of deficits approach would call for repeated practice with flash cards until this skill was mastered.

This model for teaching a skill that is not possessed by children with learning disabilities and other disorders of neuropsychological origin seems to make sense. However, the dysfunction inherent in the condition may make acquisition of the skill unusually difficult or even impossible. To illustrate, assume that a remediation of deficits approach is utilized with the child mentioned above who is unable to identify 50 Dolch sight words. After a week of direct instruction, 30 minutes per day, of flash card drill, there is no progress. Concluding that insufficient practice has been provided, the clinician increases the time on task to two 30-minute sessions per day. After another week, the child still has shown no improvement in word recognition using flash cards. As a result of neuropsychological evaluation, some evidence suggesting a learning disability that may interfere with the child's ability to acquire sight words via flash card drill is identified. The neurological report and supporting neuropsychological test data suggest dysfunction of the occipital region of the cortex: the child is cortically blind. Obviously, regardless of the hours and years devoted to flash card drill, the youngster does not possess the neurologic capacity to acquire the desired skill.

Although this example borders on the absurd, the association of other, more subtle learning disabilities with neuropsychological dysfunction similarly impedes the effectiveness of certain intervention approaches. The auditory-phonetic dyslexic, for example, may be unable to identify subtle differences in vowel sounds, so that the correct discrimination of *mitt, mutt,* and *met* is as much a gamble for this youngster as identifying words on flash cards is for the cortically blind child. Similarly, any teacher who has ever taught a dysgraphic child can attest to the futility of direct instruction; despite years of cursive writing "practice" (which the youngster might rather label "torture"), the dysgraphic child shows little improvement in handwriting quality.

Thus while a remediation of deficits approach probably is viable for children without neurologic dysfunction, at best it may be ineffective and at worst traumatizing for children with learning disabilities and other disorders of neurologic origin. For such youngsters, giving them more of something they cannot do not only fails to produce the desired learning effect, but also serves as a regular reminder of their weakest performance areas. The following two alternative approaches to intervention are preferred for such children.

A second major approach to educational intervention is the *capitalization of strengths* model (Cronbach & Snow, 1977), which calls for the utilization of the student's existing skills in developing deficient areas. Through comprehensive neuropsychological evaluation, processing strengths and weaknesses are identified. Intervention strategies are then designed to emphasize the child's strengths during the instruction of basic skills. For example, in the case of the auditory-phonetic dyslexic, a capitalization of strengths model would rely on relatively intact skills, such as whole-word, look-say approaches to sight word acquisition, and chunking or clustering prefixes, suffixes, and root words into units as cues to word recognition. Remediation strategies that emphasize weaknesses, such as auditory-phonetic approaches to word recognition, would be avoided.

The third model of educational intervention is called the *compensatory* approach (Cronbach & Snow, 1977). This technique calls for teaching strategies that circumvent the child's weaknesses and help the child achieve major objectives despite deficiencies. Such an approach is particularly applicable to populations of children with neuropsychological dysfunction, because training or retraining of skills may not be viable options. Compensatory approaches often use devices such as calculators, tape recorders, and typewriters. For example, a child with a learning disability involving mathematics calculation could succeed at working applied arithmetic problems by using a calculator or a table of arithmetic facts.

We (Hartlage & Telzrow, 1983) have developed a model of educational intervention for learning disabled children that combines models two (capitalization of strengths) and three (compensatory). This model, called the *capitalization of strengths continuum*, is designed to maximize learning potential for LD children who can master learning tasks successfully, while insuring that those with the severest learning disabilities are provided opportunities to achieve functional skills. The two extreme points on the capitalization of strengths continuum are described below.

The extreme left end of the continuum is likely to be most appropriate for children with the mildest expressions of learning disabilities, as well as some extremely bright youngsters with somewhat more serious learning problems. *Strength-matched teaching*, in which instructional methods emphasize neuropsychological strengths, is a viable approach for such youngsters. Because of the mildness of their condition, or because they are very bright and can adapt more easily, these children can utilize strength-matched teaching approaches to acquire new skills. Such intervention approaches often can be implemented successfully within a regular classroom, or at most in a special education classroom within a regular school building; hence, this represents the least restrictive end of the continuum. The outcome for children who enter the intervention continuum at this point is often very positive, for they can acquire basic skills at levels sufficient to succeed in the educational system. They may need to repeat reading assignments to achieve comprehension and may take longer to complete written work than their nonhandicapped peers. However, their skills are sufficient for most secondary education programs. The brightest of these youngsters may have learning disabilities that are not identified until undergraduate or even graduate programs in college, when the quantity and difficulty of the required material causes their processing weaknesses to be revealed.

The other extreme of the continuum is associated with very different instructional approaches and educational outcomes. Individuals at this point on the continuum are those whose learning disabilities are so severe or pervasive that they are unable to master basic skills such as reading, math, or written language beyond rudimentary levels. Such individuals may have subnormal IQ levels and impaired ability to utilize all symbol systems; they may be unable to tell time or identify monetary values, as well as display more common problems associated with reading, math, and written language. As a result, compensatory techniques are necessary in order for them to perform activities of daily living. The long-term goal for such individuals is most aptly described as functional independence with assistive devices. Thus, although such students may not become literate or learn computation skills, if taught systematic use of compensatory strategies, they can learn to drive or use public transportation, to maintain employment successfully, and to live independently.

These two descriptions represent the extremes on the capitalization of strengths continuum and probably describe a minority of LD students. Most individuals with learning disabilities are neither as well off as those able to acquire basic skills from a strength-matched teaching approach, nor as disadvantaged as those requiring a total compensatory model. Therefore, the critical decision is where to enter the capitalization of strengths continuum for a given student. The following are general guidelines for making this determination.

For most young students (i.e., up to about age 12), it is appropriate to begin at the least restrictive end of the continuum. Using the neuropsychological evaluation as the blueprint for intervention, we employ instructional techniques that emphasize processing strengths and minimize weaknesses. Ongoing appraisal of student progress is critical, because evidence of minimal or no growth may indicate the need to move to a more restrictive point on the continuum, where greater use is made of compensatory techniques. After a period of compensatory instruction with younger children, we may reintroduce strength-matched teaching approaches, because neuromaturation may allow for the acquisition of basic skills that could not be mastered earlier. However, educators should be cautioned about persisting with strength-matched teaching approaches in the face of consistent and ongoing lack of pupil progress. Such perseveration on instruction of basic skills, despite the use of strength-matched teaching methodology, may delay the introduction of compensatory teaching approaches to the point where functional living skills are compromised for children whose disabilities are severe.

For example, one young man referred to the second author for evaluation at age 16 was a virtual nonreader and had mastered only a handful of addition and subtraction facts. He could write his name, but not his address or other identifying information. He could not tell time on a nondigital watch, confused coin values, and could not read prices. And yet despite his severe, pervasive learning disabilities, his educational program each September started anew with attempts to introduce basic sight words. Compensatory techniques had not been initiated, and the young man was much more severely disabled in daily living skills than his neuropsychological profile would portend. He did not drive, had few friends, and had no productive pastimes. Following an evaluation of this young man's neuropsychological abilities, his educational program was modified to incorporate a vocational program relying on his relative strengths in right hemisphere, visuo-spatial skills, with heavy emphasis on the use of compensatory approaches and assistive devices in the acquisition of functional skills.

SPECIFIC INTERVENTION TECHNIQUES

This section will review specific intervention approaches that can maximize the learning potential of LD children. For a more comprehensive discussion of neuropsychologically based intervention with LD children, readers are referred to Telzrow and Speer (in press-a, in press-b).

Attention Deficits. In addition to the effective use of medication to enhance attention and concentration (Kavale, 1982), a variety of behavior modification approaches have been utilized with children who have attention deficits (Brown & Alford, 1984). One such approach uses a cognitive behavior modification technique, whereby children are taught to monitor their own levels of attention by periodic verbal mediation (e.g., asking themselves at cued intervals, "Am I paying attention?") (Hallahan & Sapona, 1983). Classroom alterations, such as quiet, shielded study areas, also may be useful. Instructional approaches that incorporate a series of brief lessons with varying input and output demands may maximize short attention spans (Douglas, 1983), as may breaking assignments into shorter segments, and building in a feedback system at regular intervals.

Memory Deficits. Impaired memory is a common problem in children with neuropsychological dysfunction, including learning disabled populations (Cermak, 1983; Jorm, 1983). One means of addressing this weakness is to incorporate repetition, drill, and rehearsal into instructional approaches in a systematic fashion. In addition, because learning disabled children may have particular difficulty employing rehearsal and retrieval strategies, deliberate instruction in using such techniques may be helpful (Torgesen, 1982). A variety of mnemonic aids have been successful with such populations, including the use of music or rhythm (Nocera, 1979; H. Palmer & P. Palmer, 1971) and imagery ("Federally Funded," 1984).

Reading/Spelling Disorders

Dysphonetic Dyslexic. Strategies that emphasize the orthographic, visuo-spatial features of words appear to be most beneficial in the instruction of dysphonetic dyslexics. Use of "word families" (e.g., *cat*, *rat*, *hat*, *sat*, and so forth) is one example. These can be expanded to teach multisyllabic words by "clustering" root words together with prefixes and suffixes, and using color cues to "build" new words from these component parts. Multisensory teaching strategies, which call for the child to actively visualize sound-symbol associations (e.g., "ch-" invokes the image of a speeding train), can be effective. Other strategies, such as rhythm and music, rely on the youngster's relative strengths in neuropsychological processing and have proved worthwhile. For children with the severest disorders, use of a rebus system, a nonlinguistic, pictograph approach to reading, may be desirable.

For many dyslexic children, spelling is unusually difficult. As a result, a combination of compensatory and strength-matched teaching approaches is recommended. The first step in applying this strategy involves compiling a personal list of "must be mastered" words, via input from teacher, parent, and child. The number of words may vary from 25 for young children to up to 500 or more for high school students. In addition to the obvious, frequently encountered words such as the Dolch list, the student's "must list" might include identifying information (e.g., address, birth date, school name) and terms related to the student's areas of interest or study (e.g., mechanical or sports terms). These words would be reviewed at regular intervals, and the student's weekly spelling test would be composed of 20 or so of these words, in ongoing rotation. Because experience suggests that many dyslexics can master a finite number of spelling words if rehearsed regularly, this technique incorporates the strategy of periodic review. For all other words, the student would be taught early and effective use of a spelling dictionary, moving from a picture dictionary at the earliest levels to a personal or commercially available spelling dictionary during the upper grades.

Dyseidetic Dyslexic. Instructional strategies that emphasize *phonetic* approaches to reading and spelling are favored for the child exhibiting dyseidetic or visuo-spatial dyslexia. Because such readers demonstrate a tendency to segment and decode even simple words, use of simultaneous tape recordings and written text may help avoid this tendency. Linguistic reading techniques, which emphasize the deep structure (meaning) of a passage rather than the surface structure (orthographic features), help the child develop an anticipatory approach to reading.

The spelling errors of the dyseidetic dyslexic reflect this difficulty in revisualizing common words. Words tend to be spelled phonetically correctly, although they are orthographically inaccurate. Use of sayings and spelling "rules" that provide reminders of the visuo-spatial features of phonetically irregular words (e.g., "*i* before *e* except after *c*"; "there's a *tent* at the beginning of *tentative*") may be useful for dyseidetic dyslexics. In addition, instruction in use of a spelling dictionary is recommended for these students as well.

Mixed Dyslexic. These disabled readers present an unusual instructional dilemma because they exhibit deficits in both auditory-phonetic and visuo-spatial approaches to reading. However, most mixed dyslexics demonstrate a *relative* strength in one information processing style or the other - usually in visuo-spatial ability (Telzrow et al., 1983). Once this relative strength is identified via neuropsychological evaluation, the strategies outlined above that are consistent with this profile may be employed. However, it is important to emphasize that progress in reading for the mixed dyslexic is likely to be inordinately slow, and the introduction of compensatory strategies might be considered.

Mathematics Disorders

Computation Disorders. Frequently children in this category have arithmetic disorders associated with a perceptual-organization deficit in which they exhibit number reversals and confusion of multistep mathematical processes (Rourke & Finlayson, 1978; Rourke & Strang, 1983). Often language and reasoning abilities remain intact. Intervention strategies are designed to take full advantage of these preserved abilities, while minimizing demands placed on weaker functions.

To help the child cope with directional confusion, a number line may be placed at the child's seat, with arrows demonstrating how the numerals are formed. Color coding may be used as a cue for two-digit numerals. Students are encouraged to use verbal mediation to assist with directional confusion and graph paper to aid in column alignment. Sequential steps in such arithmetic processes as multiplication and division can be summarized and coded for these children to serve as reminders in their work (Telzrow & Speer, in press-a). If mastery of basic arithmetic facts is difficult, songs or rhythm may be employed (e.g., H. Palmer & P. Palmer, 1971). For some of these children a logical system that begins with "doubles" facts (2 + 2, 3 + 3, 4 + 4, etc.) and teaches other facts through their relationship with these may be helpful (e.g., Thornton & Noxon, 1977). For those with the most severe problems, use of such assistive devices as a calculator or a table of facts is recommended.

Mathematics Reasoning. Children who exhibit deficits in mathematics reasoning often demonstrate related weaknesses in abstract reasoning and concept formation. Hence, intervention in mathematics must incorporate more comprehensive instruction in logical thinking as well.

Such instruction might use concrete objects (e.g., colors, shapes, pictures) to help children identify relationships and begin to categorize these items on the basis of their like features. A dozen blocks of various shapes, sizes, and colors, for example, can be used to help children sort on a given principle and then change set to categorize using a different system. Pictorial and verbal analogies can also be used to help identify relationships and concepts.

Summary. Intervention with learning disabled children is ideally a thoughtful and flexible process. The neuropsychological evaluation serves as the blueprint for intervention, which is designed to maximize the child's learning potential by matching teaching approaches to his or her information processing strengths. Compensatory approaches are introduced when necessary to assist children in achieving functional independence.

The following case studies illustrate how traditional psychometric measures are incorporated with specialized neuropsychological tasks to identify learning disabilities in school-aged children. Recommendations for intervention derived from these data are included for each case.

CASE STUDY #1

ATTENTION DEFICIT DISORDER WITHOUT HYPER-ACTIVITY. (Joy, white female, CA 8-9, grade 3)

Background and Observation:

Joy is a petite, bright-eyed young lady who was talkative and outgoing during the testing situation. She was referred for evaluation by her parents, who have observed unusual difficulty with school-related tasks since kindergarten or first grade.

Mr. and Mrs. T observed that Joy has trouble grasping new concepts or ideas. For example, they reported that a math assignment of 15 or 20 problems may require 1 to 1-1/2 hours to complete, even though Joy seems to be working on the task consistently. They indicated sometimes Joy may put down any answer just to complete her work. They believe that although Joy is keeping up with her class, she is struggling considerably in order to do so.

Mrs. T reported Joy was the product of an unremarkable pregnancy and delivery. Early developmental milestones were within normal limits, and her parents had no concerns until the start of school. Joy's health history has been uneventful. Although she fell out of a child's bed at approximately 2-1/2 years, her parents do not believe she bumped her head. Joy has worn glasses for amblyopia since the age of 5 years.

Joy is right-handed, as is her mother; Mr. T is left-handed. Mrs. T said she recalls having some learning problems in the early grades, although she does not believe they were as severe as Joy's seem to be. Both Mr. and Mrs. T have completed 4 years of college. Mr. T is an accountant and Mrs. T is a teacher, currently employed part-time as a substitute. Joy lives with her parents and younger sister, age 5.

Mr. and Mrs. T indicated Joy's early school experiences were not positive and that she came home from first grade crying a number of times. She had a more successful second grade year and seems more comfortable in school now. By her parent's report she sometimes has trouble falling asleep and seems to worry a lot. She is extremely fearful of animals, including larger animals like dogs, as well as insects and ants. Although they reported Joy "gets hysterical" at the sight of an animal, she has improved, and they have not been concerned about this fear.

Joy is just completing third grade in a regular classroom with approximately 15-17 children. Her teacher described Joy as quiet, timid, and well-liked by her peers. She indicated Joy requires much individual encouragement and follow-up on her work so that she does not give up. She has observed that when work becomes somewhat harder, Joy may resort to guessing in order to complete her assignment. At first when Joy was having trouble completing her seat work, she would put all her things in her book bag, as though she were finished, and sit quietly at her desk. Her teacher found that checking her work frequently was helpful, and that Joy demonstrated the ability to correct her mistakes.

On the first day of individual assessment and to a lesser degree on the second day, Joy's behavior was characterized by impulsivity, distractibility, fidgetiness, silliness, and some testing of limits. This behavior is reportedly not typical for Joy at home, and especially not in the classroom, according to her parents and teacher. On the day of the second evaluation, Joy seemed to apply monumental effort to concentrate and stay on task; although improvement was evident, she continued to demonstrate attention deficits despite frequent breaks.

Test Results:

The letter "S" is used to indicate a strength and the letter "W" to indicate a weakness represented by test scores.

Wechsler Intelligence Scale for Children-Revised (WISC-R)

Verbal	SS	Performance	SS
Information	12	Picture Completion	13
Similarities	14	Picture Arrangement	(S)15
Arithmetic	(W)9	Block Design	(W)9
Vocabulary	(S)15	Object Assembly	(W)9
Comprehension	11	Coding	14
Digit Span	(W)6		

Verbal IQ = 113   Performance IQ = 114

Full Scale IQ = 115

These results suggest Joy's intellectual ability is above average, equivalent to the 84th percentile of the general population. No significant difference was noted between her Verbal and Performance IQ scores. Four subtests were significantly depressed relative to Joy's own mean performance. Two of these four subtests - Arithmetic and Digit Span - are especially sensitive to distractibility and attention deficits. Weaknesses in Block Design and Object Assembly have been associated with deficits in perceptual organizational ability.

Woodcock-Johnson Psychoeducational Battery (WJPB) - Cognitive Scale

Cognitive Factor	SS
Verbal Ability	119
Reasoning	100
Visual-Perceptual Speed	118
Memory	84

These results reflect significant variability in Joy's performance on different types of tasks - from superior skills on verbal and speeded perceptual-motor tasks, to average reasoning skills, to significantly below average memory performance. Such a profile is consistent with observations Mr. and Mrs. T have made about Joy's difficulty grasping new concepts, as well as trouble remembering directions. The memory factor score is especially depressed by the Numbers Reversed subtest, which is likely to be vulnerable to the effects of attention deficits.

Woodcock-Johnson Psychoeducational Battery (WJPB) - Achievement Scale

Predicted achievement levels can be derived from Joy's performance on the cognitive portion of the WJPB. Expected achievement scores, as well as actual achievement levels, are as follows:

	Expected		Actual	
Cluster	SS	GE	SS	GE
Reading	107	4.1	101	3.7
Math	115	4.2	102	3.7
Written Language	114	4.3	98	3.6
Knowledge	118	5.0	113	4.7

These results suggest Joy's actual achievement levels in reading, math, and written language are all within the average range. Because expected levels are above average, her academic achievement scores are somewhat below predicted levels.

Token Test for Children

Part	SS
I	500
II	502
III	494
IV	502
V	504
Total	501

These results indicate that Joy's total score is within normal limits compared to other children her age, although her performance on subtest III was significantly below average. Joy's attention to the task varied widely, and her poor performance on this subtest could be attributed to these attention deficits.

Beery Test of Visual Motor Integration

Joy's performance resulted in a standard score of 11, which is equivalent to the 75th percentile of the standardization population.

Child Behavior Checklist-Parent Edition

Mrs. T responded to the CBCL items. According to her ratings, Joy's behavior is within normal limits relative to other girls her age.

Child Behavior Checklist-Teacher Edition

Joy's teacher's ratings of her behavior indicated it is within normal limits compared to other girls her age.

Aphasia Screening Test

Joy's performance on the AST did not demonstrate any pathognomonic signs of language-based learning disabilities.

Category Test

Because Joy is just a few months shy of her ninth birthday, the older children's version of the Category Test was administered. Joy enjoyed the task, but committed more errors than the average child of her intellectual ability level (66 errors). Even considering she is somewhat young, this number of errors may suggest difficulty with logical abstract reasoning, problem solving, and concept formation.

Finger Oscillation

Joy's scores (RH = 30 taps/10 seconds; LH = 24 taps/10 seconds) reflect depressed finger tapping on the left hand. Her pattern of scores on the Category Test and on finger tapping are consistent with the presence of mild, probably chronic neuropsychological dysfunction that may be reflected in subtle problems, such as attention deficits, problems monitoring behavior, and weaknesses in abstract reasoning and concept formation.

Summary and Recommendations:

Joy is a bright young lady who exhibits a wide range of behaviors in various settings. In school her teacher perceives her as timid and shy, and although she requires substantial teacher encouragement, she is described as an average student. This is in a setting where the mean intellectual ability level, as measured by a group test, is a standard deviation above average. At home Joy's parents do not see her as quiet or timid, but they have observed that an inordinate amount of effort is required for Joy to succeed in her school tasks. In the context of individual testing conducted by different examiners on different occasions, Joy's behavior is characterized by distractibility, impulsivity, and some oppositional behavior. It was reported by Joy's parents and teacher that she may "tune out" when work gets difficult, resorting to guessing in order to complete the task; this was observed during individual testing as well.

Current testing suggests Joy's behavior is consistent with the presence of an attention deficit disorder, a condition associated with mild, chronic neuropsychological dysfunction. For Joy, most of the time (e.g., in the classroom) this condition occurs without hyperactivity, although she may have more than the usual amount of difficulty following directions and working through a task. When the pressure increases - such as during group or individual testing - Joy may "tune out" (e.g., mark any answer on the group test, as her teacher observed) or exhibit overt signs of distress such as fidgetiness, impulsivity, testing of limits, and so on, as observed during individual testing.

In addition to signs of an attention deficit disorder, current testing suggests a neuropsychological weakness in abstract reasoning, concept formation, and similar higher order cognitive skills. Hence despite Joy's superior verbal skills, she has difficulty understanding and applying abstract ideas. At this stage of her educational career, these difficulties may be most evident in her understanding of mathematics concepts.

Joy's problems are subtle yet nevertheless quite real, and are consistent with her parents' observations of her difficulties. Such problems are sometimes referred to as "general learning disabilities," in that these are subtle problems of attention and learning that may impact a number of areas. This is to be distinguished from "specific learning disabilities," which refers to unique deficits in reading, math, or language.

The following approaches might be explored to mitigate the potential negative effects of Joy's difficulties:

1. The establishment of a classroom environment that is characterized by brief, varying lessons and short assignments with frequent opportunities for feedback;
2. The use of cognitive behavior modification - a "self-talk" approach in which Joy can be taught to monitor her own attention at regular intervals and to persist on difficult tasks;
3. The presentation of systematic instruction in abstract reasoning and concept formation, beginning with such elements as observing similarities, categorizing, and moving to application and generalization; and
4. The exploration, with Joy's pediatrician, of the possible advantages and disadvantages of a trial of an appropriate pharmacological approach such as Ritalin.

CASE STUDY #2

AUDITORY-PHONETIC DYSLEXIA.
(Sean, white male, CA 10-9, grade 4)

Background Information:

School officials requested a second opinion evaluation for Sean to help determine whether his current special education placement is appropriate. Sean is the younger of Mrs. M's sons. Sean's father had a history of social problems, according to Mrs. M: he completed the 11th grade in school, was rejected for military service, and was unable to maintain a job. Mr. M committed suicide in 1979, some time after he was separated from Sean's mother.

Mrs. M noted that Sean was the product of an uneventful pregnancy, but a long, difficult labor and delivery. She was told he lacked sufficient oxygen for a time. According to his mother Sean was unusually active from birth and rarely slept more than an hour at a time. At age 4, at the suggestion of her pediatrician, Sean was started on Cylert, and some time later this was changed to Ritalin, which he has taken since. Mrs. M reported Sean takes 20 mg of time-release Ritalin twice per day, in the morning and at noon. She feels this has had positive effects on his behavior.

According to Mrs. M, Sean has always had learning and behavior problems. School difficulties were noted in kindergarten. He repeated first grade, and was placed in a special education program during his second year in first grade. Mrs. M said Sean has great difficulty sitting still, has "good days and bad days," and is sometimes defiant and belligerent. Mrs. M noted Sean has a low self-esteem, and frequently refers to himself as "retarded" or "dumb."

Sean spends most of his day in a learning disability classroom, although he is mainstreamed for nonacademic subjects. His teachers have identified these behaviors as those which interfere most with his learning: (a) distractibility - off-task behavior; (b) interrupting, talking out inappropriately; (c) leaving his seat inappropriately; (d) not persisting in doing work when it becomes difficult; and (e) mumbling to himself. They have observed that allowing Sean to choose within a set of options is an effective strategy for insuring he does his work without a great deal of fuss.

Observation and Test Results:

Although it had been reported that Sean often rejects strangers, he willingly accompanied the examiner on two occasions and cooperated well during a very long (2-1/2 hours) test session. He is an attractive, well-groomed 10-year-old who seems to be large for his age. No obvious physical anomalies were noted. Sean was observed to "play" with objects on the table (e.g., a car he brought with him), although this habit did not appear to distract him, and he did not protest when, on occasion, he was asked to put these objects away. Sean did not demonstrate frustration or refusal on tasks, even those that were hard for him. Test results would appear to be a valid estimate of Sean's current functioning levels.

Wechsler Intelligence Scale for Children-Revised (WISC-R)

Verbal	SS	Performance	SS
Information	(W)6	Picture Completion	12
Similarities	9	Picture Arrangement	(S)14
Arithmetic	(W)6	Block Design	(S)14
Vocabulary	9	Object Assembly	(S)19
Comprehension	(W)7	Coding	(W)6
Digit Span	(W)4		

Verbal IQ = 84   Performance IQ = 121

Full Scale IQ = 99

Although these results reflect average intellectual ability overall, a significant difference is observed between Sean's Verbal and Performance IQ scores. A difference of this magnitude occurs in fewer than .01% of the WISC-R standardization sample. The range of Sean's subtest scores reflects significant variability, resulting in a Selz-Reitan scatter index of 1.6. A scatter index of this magnitude occurs in fewer than 1% of white students at this IQ level and indicates probable neurological dysfunction.

When WISC-R subtest scores are recategorized according to Bannatyne's specifications, it is apparent that spatial abilities comprise a significant strength ($M = 15$) and sequential abilities a significant weakness ($M = 5$). This pattern is consistent with a neuropsychological processing disorder involving sequential, linguistic abilities.

Kaufman Assessment Battery for Children (K-ABC)

Sequential	SS	Simultaneous	SS
Hand Movements	9	Gestalt Closure	(S)13
Number Recall	7	Triangles	(S)11
Word Order	6	Matrix Analogies	6
		Spatial Memory	7
		Photo Series	7

Sequential Score = 83±8   Simultaneous Score = 91±6

Mental Processing Composite = 86±6

These results reflect somewhat lower intellectual ability than demonstrated by the WISC-R. Although the 8-point difference between the Sequential and Simultaneous processing scales is not statistically significant, strengths for Sean were noted on two Simultaneous subtests: Gestalt Closure and Triangles. Such a pattern is consistent with the V<P and sequential<spatial patterns exhibited on the WISC-R.

K-ABC Achievement Tests

Subtest	SS	GE
Faces & Places	(S)96±8	
Arithmetic	79±8	2.9
Riddles	89±9	
Reading/Decoding	76±8	2.6
Reading/Understanding	77±8	2.6

These results indicate that Sean's achievement levels in reading and arithmetic are significantly below his present grade placement. One subtest, Faces & Places, a general information, incidental learning task, represented a significant strength for Sean. The pattern of scores demonstrated on the K-ABC is similar to the customary pattern of scores reported for learning disabled children. This pattern is characterized by a higher Simultaneous than Sequential Score; strength in Gestalt Closure; best achievement performance on Riddles; and a tendency to score most poorly on Sequential subtests. It should be noted that at least some groups of LD children score as poorly on Simultaneous subtests with high Sequential components (e.g., Matrix Analogies, Spatial Memory, and Photo Series) as on Sequential subtests. This was true of Sean's performance.

Boder Test of Reading/Spelling Patterns

Sean's reading quotient on the Boder is 68, which represents a significant reading deficit. He spelled 40% of the known words (i.e., words he read) correctly, and none of the unknown words as good phonic equivalents. This pattern is consistent with the test authors' criteria defining dysphonetic dyslexia.

Finger Oscillation

Though the level of Sean's performance (RH = 39 taps/10 seconds; LH = 41 taps/10 seconds) is within normal limits for his age, the pattern of performance is highly unusual. Although Sean is right-handed, he demonstrated faster left-hand tapping speed. This pattern of depressed right-hand tapping speed relative to left is consistent with neuropsychological dysfunction implicating the left cerebral hemisphere. This hypothesis is consistent with performance patterns on the WISC-R, the K-ABC, and the Boder.

Trail Making Test

Sean's performance (Trails A = 23 seconds; Trails B = 58 seconds) was significantly slower than would be predicted, consistent with evidence of neuropsychological dysfunction.

Aphasia Screening Test

Sean made a number of errors on the AST, including dysnomia (called triangle "rectangle"), spelling dyspraxia (square/sa, triangle/r, clock/colke, he shouted the waring/sar), dyscalculia (85 - 27 = couldn't compute, 17 x 3 written as 17 + 3 = couldn't compute). These results are consistent with other indications of a severe learning disability in the areas of reading, writing, and arithmetic.

Devereux Elementary School Behavior Rating Scale

Sean's teacher completed the Devereux items. Her ratings indicated that Sean's behavior is significantly different from his peers' on 15 of the 16 scales. Six scales were more than two standard deviations above the mean: socially withdrawn, failure anxiety, blaming, irrelevant thinking/talking, negative/aggressive, and inattention. This pattern of scores illustrates the serious concern about behavior described by Sean's teachers, and suggests that his behavior has an adverse effect on his educational progress.

Child Behavior Checklist-Parent Edition

Mrs. M responded to the items on the CBCL. Her ratings indicated that three scales were significantly above average when compared with other boys Sean's age: Depressed (T = 85), Social Withdrawal (T = 73), and Aggressive (T = 73). These results support Sean's teacher's observations that, relative to other boys his age, Sean demonstrates more significant behavior disorders in both acting out and withdrawing.

Summary and Recommendations:

Sean is an attractive, sturdy young man who has a history of learning and behavior problems. Current test results indicate the presence of a significant learning disability. This disability is reflected in serious problems with reading, spelling, written expression, and arithmetic. There is evidence this disability is due to associated neuropsychological dysfunction.

In addition to a specific learning disability, Sean's teachers and mother have identified serious behavior disorders. Sean is reported to be extremely unhappy and depressed, to have low frustration tolerance, low self-esteem, and high levels of hostility. When thwarted, he becomes very angry and sometimes is belligerent and aggressive.

It is likely Sean's learning and behavior problems are interrelated. Increasing evidence suggests that boys with behavior disorders have increased incidence of neuropsychological deficits. This may suggest that Sean is, by temperament, more likely to exhibit behavior problems. In addition, it is likely that his learning disability has exacerbated many of the problems noted.

These results suggest that Sean would benefit from an educational program that is as follows:

1. Highly structured, with consistent feedback relative to appropriate and inappropriate behavior;
2. Designed to Sean's style of learning, including emphasis on pictures, projects, and other instructional strategies with a highly visuo-spatial orientation;
3. Helpful in enabling Sean to increase his tolerance for frustration, accept himself better, and produce more adaptive behaviors with others; and

4. Able to expose Sean to career exploration in areas where he might experience eventual success, such as vocational areas emphasizing perceptual organization abilities.

CASE STUDY #3

VISUO-SPATIAL DYSLEXIC SPELLING PATTERN. (Sally, white female, CA 10-6, grade 5)

Background Information:

Sally is an attractive, slightly chubby youngster who was generally pleasant and cooperative throughout several test sessions with two different examiners. She was referred for evaluation by her mother, who indicated she has been concerned about Sally's academic progress since approximately first grade. Although Sally's progress reports were satisfactory, Mrs. G observed that Sally had difficulty developing early reading skills and had trouble concentrating in the classroom. She has continued to be concerned that despite Sally's progress in her school work, it seems very difficult for her. Mrs. G also noted that Sally's group test scores were low, and that her teacher indicated she tried to help her but was not sure what to do. Mrs. G has observed that Sally may lose her place when reading; she transposes letters in spelling, even when copying from correctly spelled text; and she loses answers on the page when there is a lot of printed material.

Mrs. G indicated Sally was the product of a normal pregnancy. At approximately 2 weeks of age, Sally developed feeding problems, with vomiting. Her formula was adjusted with good results. Mrs. G also noted that Sally has continued to have a "sensitive stomach," and occasionally may miss school as a result of these episodes, which she suspects may be stress-related. Sally has no known allergies. Night terrors developed at about 18 months of age and have continued to the present, although their frequency has dropped off greatly, and Sally has not had an episode for about a year.

Mrs. G indicated she and her husband and Sally are right-handed; Sally's sister, grade 8, is left-handed. Mrs. G seemed unaware of any learning problems in the family, but then described herself as a "terrible speller."

She views Sally as having a lot of common sense, but not devoting much time to her school work lately.

Test Results:

Wechsler Intelligence Scale for Children-Revised (WISC-R)

Verbal	SS	Performance	SS
Information	10	Picture Completion	10
Similarities	(S)14	Picture Arrangement	10
Arithmetic	12	Block Design	(W)8
Vocabulary	12	Object Assembly	10
Comprehension	(S)17	Coding	11
Digit Span	9		

Verbal IQ = 118   Performance IQ = 98

Full Scale IQ = 109

Although Sally's overall intellectual ability is within the high average range, a significant difference exists between her Verbal and Performance IQ scores. Approximately 10% of children Sally's age show a V-P discrepancy of this magnitude. This pattern of scores indicates that Sally's school-related verbal skills are significantly better developed than her perceptual organizational ability. Analysis of Sally's WISC-R scores according to Bannatyne's recategorization model reveals her relative strength in verbal conceptual abilities (M = 14). Her lowest mean score was for spatial abilities (M = 9), suggesting that pure perceptual, visuo-spatial tasks are relatively difficult for Sally.

Kaufman Assessment Battery for Children (K-ABC)

Sequential	SS	Simultaneous	SS
Hand Movements	9	Gestalt Closure	11
Number Recall	10	Triangles	10
Word Order	9	Matrix Analogies	10
		Spatial Memory	12
		Photo Series	10

Sequential Score = 95±8   Simultaneous Score = 104±6

Mental Processing Composite = 100±6

Achievement Subtests	SS
Faces & Places	114±8
Arithmetic	114±8
Riddles	111±9
Reading/Decoding	(W)97±8
Reading/Understanding	105±8
Total	109±4

These results present a somewhat different pattern of scores than observed on the WISC-R, with no significant strengths or weaknesses noted on the mental processing subtests. Sally's achievement test results are generally above average except for the Reading/Decoding subtest, which represents a significant weakness compared to Sally's own mean performance. This pattern suggests relatively more difficulty with sight word identification, consistent with Sally's V>P and sequential>spatial profile on the WISC-R.

Boder Test of Reading/Spelling Patterns

Although Sally's reading quotient was within the average range (107), she exhibited some spelling difficulty, correctly spelling only 50% of known words and 70% of unknown words as GFEs. This is consistent with errors observed in a dyseidetic or visuo-spatial dyslexic, and suggests that Sally relies on an auditory-phonetic approach to reading and spelling and may experience difficulty with spelling phonetically irregular words correctly. This difficulty with the orthographic characteristics of spelling words is consistent with her relative personal weakness in spatial processing on the WISC-R, as well as the weakness observed in Reading/Decoding on the K-ABC.

Test of Written Language (TOWL)

Subtest	SS	GE
Vocabulary	14	>9.0
Thematic Maturity	12	8.9
Spelling	9	4.7
Word Usage	10	7.0
Style	10	5.7
Thought Units	11	
Handwriting	13	

Sally's strong vocabulary subtest score on the TOWL is compatible with her superior verbal conceptual ability on the WISC-R. Spelling was her lowest score on the TOWL, consistent with her pattern of scores on the WISC-R and the Boder.

Halstead Category Test

Sally's performance on the Category Test (74 errors) suggests difficulty with concept formation and abstract reasoning utilizing visuo-spatial stimuli. This does not appear to have affected performance in related subject areas (e.g., arithmetic) to date.

Aphasia Screening Test

Sally had moderate difficulty with the drawings on the AST, and also made errors in computation and spelling. This error pattern suggests mild neuropsychological impairment involving visuo-spatial skills and subtle language ability implicating spelling and orthographic features of words.

Trail Making Test

Although Sally's performance on Trails A (25 seconds) was somewhat slower than age expectancy, her performance on Trails B (32 seconds) was within normal limits.

Finger Oscillation

Sally's level of performance is within normal limits for her age (RH = 43 taps/10 seconds; LH = 36 taps/10 seconds), although the irregular pattern reveals depressed left-hand tapping speed relative to right. This pattern is consistent with the visuo-spatial difficulties she has demonstrated on the WISC-R, Boder, K-ABC reading/decoding, and other neuropsychological tests.

Summary and Recommendations:

Results of cognitive, achievement, and neuropsychological assessment suggest a mild chronic impairment likely to be reflected in subtle visuo-spatial weaknesses such as letter or number reversals and poor spelling, especially of phonetically irregular words. Despite these difficulties,

Sally has compensated well in maintaining academic achievement appropriate for her age and level of mental ability. Although the observations Mrs. G has made about Sally's learning are consistent with her pattern of neuropsychological strengths and weaknesses, her problems are relatively subtle and do not appear to warrant special education assistance.

The following suggestions may facilitate Sally's academic progress:

1. As often as possible, attempt to utilize a multisensory approach; aural instructions used to supplement visual directions may prove helpful.
2. Present Sally with printed materials that are clear, neat, and uncrowded. Excessively small type may be more difficult for her to process.
3. Consider separate spelling and content grades in subject areas such as science and social studies.
4. Explore the development and use of a personal spelling dictionary.
5. Use compensatory strategies for minimizing the effects of her visuo-spatial weakness, such as a place marker when reading, additional time for copying from chalkboard, and so forth.
6. Investigate the possibility of systematic instruction in logical reasoning and problem solving. As Sally progresses through the grades and increased demands are placed on abstract reasoning and concept formation, she may begin to experience difficulty (e.g., high error score on Category Test).

CASE STUDY #4

MIXED DYSLEXIA. (Jerry, black male, CA 11-9, grade 5)

Background and Observation:

Jerry is an attractive, neatly and modishly dressed youngster who has received learning disabilities instruction in reading and language arts for the past 3 years. His teachers are concerned about his lack of progress despite this intervention, and requested this evaluation to assist in planning an appropriate educational program for him.

Mrs. D indicated her pregnancy and delivery were normal and that Jerry's early motor milestones were on schedule, although he was somewhat slow to talk. He attended a preschool program at age 4 and got along fairly well, although Mrs. D recalled the teacher had said he "liked to play." He had difficulty in kindergarten, was placed in first grade, and then retained there. He has been placed in each grade subsequently.

Mrs. D recognizes Jerry's difficulty with reading and language, but she does not have difficulty understanding his speech. She described Jerry as a responsible youngster who often reminded her he had homework to do. He is successful at a number of activities that Mrs. D recalls her daughters did not attempt until they were much older, such as cooking. She noted that Jerry is also very good at building things and figuring out how things work. He has had no significant illnesses or injuries, has no allergies, and is on no medication.

Mr. and Mrs. D each completed high school. Mrs. D reported there is no history of learning problems in the family. Both parents and all three children are right-handed.

Jerry's LD teacher instructs him in reading and language arts. She is concerned that he has made very little progress in reading. She has not been able to observe a consistent error pattern that would assist her in developing an intervention plan. Although Jerry is generally pleasant and cooperative, his teacher reported he may try to avoid tasks he finds especially difficult, such as written language tasks. She also has observed that Jerry has difficulty remembering and integrating information he hears, so her use of taped material has not been entirely successful.

Jerry's regular fifth grade teacher described him as responsible and conscientious. She feels he is good in math, but is concerned because his reading is so poor that he cannot read story problems. She noted that he sometimes has a short attention span and is easily distracted. Both teachers reported Jerry's difficulty concentrating in a group and working independently. He seeks a great deal of adult direction in completing tasks.

The speech pathologist who evaluated Jerry reported that his speech tends to be garbled, but when he concentrates he seems to speak more clearly. His oral structures appear to be intact.

Jerry was evaluated at school over 3 days. Initially he appeared somewhat shy, uncomfortable, and perhaps a bit sullen; he did not make eye contact or initiate conversation, and often sighed, yawned, or made other gestures of impatience. Much of this behavior seemed to be of a testing, almost bluffing nature, and he became increasingly comfortable as time went along. In general Jerry appeared to use maximum effort on the tasks presented, and test results appear to reflect current performance levels accurately.

Test Results:

Wechsler Intelligence Scale for Children-Revised (WISC-R)

Verbal	SS	Performance	SS
Information	(W)4	Picture Completion	(S)13
Similarities	(S)12	Picture Arrangement	(S)13
Arithmetic	8	Block Design	8
Vocabulary	7	Object Assembly	9
Comprehension	10	Coding	(W)7
Digit Span	7		

Verbal IQ = 88   Performance IQ = 100

Full Scale IQ = 92

These results suggest that Jerry's overall intellectual ability is within the low average range, consistent with previous findings. His verbal ability is somewhat lower than nonverbal ability, although a V-P difference of this magnitude is not unusual. According to Bannatyne's recategorization system, Jerry shows relative strengths on spatial (M = 10) and verbal conceptualization (M = 10), with comparative weaknesses in sequential (M = 7) and acquired knowledge (M = 6). These results suggest that Jerry generally will have greater difficulty processing information in a sequential, linguistic mode than in a holistic, visuo-spatial manner.

Kaufman Assessment Battery for Children (K-ABC)

Sequential	SS	Simultaneous	SS
Hand Movements	7	Gestalt Closure	7
Number Recall	7	Triangles	8
Word Order	7	Matrix Analogies	10

Sequential	SS	Simultaneous	SS
		Spatial Memory	9
		Photo Series	(S)11

Sequential Score = 81±9   Simultaneous Score = 93±7

Mental Processing Composite = 86±6

Although somewhat lower than the WISC-R (probably as a result of more recent standardization), these scores demonstrate a similar pattern of information processing. They reflect Jerry's greater difficulty processing linear, sequential information than solving problems relying to a greater degree on simultaneous, gestalt processing.

K-ABC Achievement Tests

Subtests	SS
Faces & Places	76±9
Arithmetic	(S)98±8
Riddles	(S)102±9
Reading/Decoding	(W)<50±8
Reading/Understanding	(W)55±9
Total	73±4

The Achievement subtests on the K-ABC demonstrate the severe difficulty Jerry has in reading. Although Arithmetic and Riddles represent significant strengths, both the reading subtests are severely depressed.

Jerry's profile on the K-ABC is somewhat consistent with the pattern for LD children. This profile is characterized by a higher Simultaneous than Sequential score, strength on Gestalt Closure, Riddles representing highest achievement subtest, and generally lower performance on Sequential subtests. It is important to note that Jerry's highest achievement subtest, Riddles, is a listening task requiring integration of information. It has the highest simultaneous loading of any of the achievement tests and although it is language-related, reflects Jerry's relative strength in this area.

Boder Test of Reading/Spelling Patterns

Jerry obtained a reading quotient of 53 on the Boder; he was able to spell 100% of the known words (i.e., words read) correctly, and was unable to produce a single good phonic equivalent (GFE) on unknown words. According to the criteria outlined in the manual, Jerry's pattern of scores on the Boder is consistent with a mixed dyslexic reading pattern, indicating he has difficulty with both the visuo-spatial, orthographic features of written language and the auditory-phonetic aspects of reading. However, Jerry's spelling pattern suggests relatively greater difficulty with auditory-phonetic skills, such as phoneme-grapheme associations and sound blending. Although Jerry may have success at associating sounds and symbols in isolation, applying these skills in an automatic, routine fashion may be quite difficult.

Category Test

Jerry's error score, 31, was well within normal limits for his age, and suggests no deficits in abstract reasoning and concept formation. This score suggests his learning disabilities are fairly discrete in their relationship to language-related skills, rather than reflecting pervasive deficits in higher cognitive processes. Jerry's average score on the Category test is no doubt associated with his relative strength in mathematics.

Trail Making Test

Jerry's performance on this task was somewhat slower than age expectancy levels, indicating possible mild impairment on this task (Trails A = 16 seconds; Trails B = 46 seconds).

Aphasia Screening Test

Jerry committed a number of pathognomonic errors, including dysnomic errors (called cross "triangle," then corrected to "X"; called triangle "square, I mean triangle"). He made numerous spelling errors (square/quld, cross/quoff, triangle/yanlg), and demonstrated evidence of both dyslexia and dysarthria. Jerry's pattern of errors on the AST is consistent with the learning difficulties observed in school and on psychometric tests.

Finger Oscillation

Jerry's tapping speed on both hands was significantly depressed, showing generalized motor impairment (RH =

34 taps/10 seconds; LH = 31 taps/10 seconds). Such a pattern is consistent with the kind of expressive speech disorders Jerry demonstrates (e.g., word finding problems, dysarthria).

Child Behavior Checklist-Teacher Edition

Both Jerry's regular and LD teachers responded to the CBCL items regarding possible problem behaviors. Both teachers rated Jerry's behavior within normal limits compared with other boys his age.

Child Behavior Checklist-Parent Edition

Mrs. D's response to the parent version of the CBCL also indicated Jerry's behavior to be within normal limits for boys his age.

Summary and Recommendations:

Jerry is an attractive, spirited young man who demonstrates a fair amount of testing behavior but is generally cooperative with an accepting, tolerant adult. He is somewhat distractible, has difficulty completing independent work, and requires considerable adult attention. However, neither his teachers nor his mother rated Jerry's behavior as significantly different from his same-age peers.

Testing demonstrates the presence of pervasive language-related learning disabilities observed in garbled, dysarthric speech, word-finding problems, extreme reading and spelling problems, and associated difficulty in producing written language. These difficulties appear to have neuropsychological origin, resulting in a specific pattern of deficits that are highly resistant to remediation, despite the best efforts of Jerry and his teachers. Testing suggests Jerry's nonverbal reasoning is within normal limits, and his math computation and reasoning appear to be adequate, as long as he is not required to read when solving problems.

The nature and degree of Jerry's neuropsychologically based language problems suggest that he will require significant adjustments in his educational program throughout his school career. Although both orthographic and auditory phonetic aspects of reading and spelling are difficult for Jerry, the former represents a somewhat stronger processing mode. Hence a whole-word, visuo-spatial, clustering approach to reading and spelling instruction may be relatively more successful, with emphasis on multisensory, integrated, repetitive intervention approaches.

It is likely Jerry's progress in reading and written language areas will be extremely slow. As a result, modified expectations and an emphasis on compensatory strategies are recommended. It is especially important that his impaired reading skills do not interfere with his progress in other areas of success (e.g., math). As Jerry gets older, he also will benefit from pre-vocational and vocational counseling by professionals sensitive to the special needs of dyslexic children.

CASE STUDY #5

DYSGRAPHIA AND SPELLING DYSPRAXIA WITHOUT DYSLEXIA. (Kurt, white male, CA 11-1, grade 5)

Background and Observation:

Kurt is a mature, articulate, sandy-haired 11-year-old who has just completed the fourth grade and will be entering fifth grade in the fall. He wears glasses and appears to be physically sturdy and agile. Kurt lives with his parents and older sister, age 16.

Kurt's mother indicated she was concerned about him as a preschooler, when he avoided pencil and paper activities. He had amblyopia, and his eye was patched at that time, so she attributed his avoidance of such activities to this. Although he seemed a bit slower to read than his peers, by mid-first or early second grade his reading and math skills were good. He demonstrated unique difficulty with spelling and handwriting, which continue to represent major educational problems.

Mrs. L indicated her pregnancy and delivery were normal. Both parents described Kurt as "colicky" for the first several months, and Mr. L recalled that as a young child Kurt hated to ride in a car, and screamed and cried when this was necessary.

Mrs. L reported a family history of learning problems. Her mother (Kurt's maternal grandmother) was described as a "terrible speller," and Mrs. L's two brothers had degrees of reading and spelling problems, one of them severe. One of these brothers was left-handed, as is Kurt;

both parents are right-handed. Both parents have college degrees. Mrs. L is a teacher, and Mr. L is an attorney.

Kurt's parents described him as mature and responsible. He is successful at several physical/athletic activities, has many friends, and seems to be well-liked. They are concerned that as he gets older, increasing demands for written work may cause Kurt to become frustrated. They requested this evaluation to determine if other interventions may be available for Kurt.

Kurt's regular fourth grade teacher indicated he was a strong reader who was verbal and well-respected by his peers. He avoided writing tasks, but she arranged for an older student to transcribe Kurt's dictated work, and this was successful. His teacher indicated Kurt made many spelling errors, and seemed unable to retain these words for any length of time, even after spelling them successfully on a spelling test.

Kurt has received LD tutoring and supplemental speech therapy for spelling assistance for approximately 2 years. His LD tutor indicated Kurt may be distracted when another student is present. She has noted better results when visual cues are used to rehearse spelling words, although long-term retention is very limited.

Kurt was cooperative and talkative during the evaluation. Although his mother reported he may have been a bit resistant about the testing, once the purpose for assessment was explained, Kurt seemed content and motivated to do well. Current test results appear to be an accurate reflection of Kurt's current performance.

Test Results:

Wechsler Intelligence Scale for Children-Revised (WISC-R)

Verbal	SS	Performance	SS
Information	13	Picture Completion	12
Similarities	(S)18	Picture Arrangement	16
Arithmetic	(W)11	Block Design	14
Vocabulary	16	Object Assembly	12
Comprehension	(S)18	Coding	(W)11
Digit Span	15		

Verbal IQ = 133   Performance IQ = 121

Full Scale IQ = 130

Kurt's general intellectual ability is within the superior range, equivalent to the 98th percentile of the general population. Although all subtest scores are within the average range or above, Kurt demonstrates a relative weakness on two subtests - Arithmetic and Coding - that are reported to be sensitive to learning disabilities in children. Recategorization of WISC-R scores according to Bannatyne reveals greatest strengths in verbal conceptualization ($M = 17$), with somewhat lower mean scores on both spatial (13) and sequential (12) factors.

Test of Written Language (TOWL)

Subtest	SS	GE
Vocabulary	14	>9.0
Thematic Maturity	9	4.6
Spelling	6	2.0
Word Usage	10	7.0
Style	10	6.2
Thought Units	6	2.7
Handwriting	4	<2.3

These results indicate that three subtests - Spelling, Thought Units, and Handwriting - are significantly below average for Kurt's age and ability. It is clear Kurt has unusual difficulty with written language tasks. He tends to print and must be encouraged to write in cursive. His printing is very primitive and resembles that of a 7-year-old child. These mechanical skills are in contrast to age appropriate or above performance in vocabulary, word usage, and style.

Boder Test of Reading/Spelling Patterns

Kurt performed in a superior fashion on the reading portion of the Boder, with a reading quotient of 131, consistent with his level of intellectual ability. Spelling performance, however, revealed severe impairment in spelling both known (i.e., words read correctly) and unknown words. Kurt did not spell any of the known words correctly and was able to spell only 10% of the unknown words as good phonic equivalents. Kurt's pattern of errors is characteristic of a severe spelling dyspraxia. He has difficulty making sound-symbol associations, and his spelling errors seemed to be characterized by orthographic/configuration similarities (e.g., human/hemen, tomato/tometoe, beauty/bouty). A similar reliance on the orthographic features of words was observed in Kurt's reading substitution errors (lame/lime, monument/moment, population/pollution). It is likely Kurt self-corrects these errors when reading in context.

Kurt's performance on the Boder confirms the presence of severe spelling disorders characterized by difficulty associating sounds and symbols and remembering familiar words. Kurt probably is unable to sequence and blend sounds in the spelling process, and hence reliance on a phonetic code for spelling would not be helpful. Although his ability to recall whole-word orthographic configurations is somewhat better, his spelling accuracy is limited to words much below his reading level.

Trail Making Test

Kurt's performance was within normal limits on Trails A (12 seconds), but somewhat slower on Trails B (45 seconds), where mean performance time for boys is 38 seconds. This performance is consistent with possible neuropsychological dysfunction.

Name Writing

This task requires the child to write his name with the dominant and nondominant hand. Performance is timed, and the speeds of the two hands are compared. The pattern of Kurt's performance, with essentially identical performance times on the two hands, is indicative of possible neuropsychological dysfunction.

Aphasia Screening Test

Kurt made numerous errors on the AST, including constructional dyspraxia, spelling dyspraxia, dysgraphia, and left-right confusion. These errors are consistent with a pattern of neuropsychologically based disorders of written language and spelling.

Sensory Perceptual Examination

Kurt's performance resulted in some right-sided suppression on simultaneous hand-face stimulation. This pattern of performance is consistent with impaired left cerebral hemisphere functioning suggested by Kurt's performance on other tasks.

Finger Oscillation

Although the level of Kurt's performance is within normal limits for his age (LH = 42 taps/10 seconds; RH = 33 taps/10 seconds), the disparity between his two hands is atypical. Depressed right-hand tapping relative to left is consistent with dysfunction of the left hemisphere, indicated by Kurt's pattern of learning disabilities.

Child Behavior Checklist-Parent Edition

Mrs. L responded to the CBCL items; her ratings indicated Kurt's behavior is within normal limits when compared with other boys his age.

Clinical Impressions

Kurt demonstrates some dysmorphic features that may indicate the presence of neurodevelopmental problems, including epicanthal folds and a curved fifth digit on his left hand. He is orally articulate and obviously bright and curious. He is clearly aware of his unique difficulty with spelling and writing and seems a bit embarrassed by these problems. He appears to be a mature 11-year-old who demonstrates typical pre-adolescent tendencies to assert himself.

Summary and Recommendations:

Present testing and information from Kurt's teachers and parents suggest chronic neuropsychological impairment reflected in spelling dyspraxia and dysgraphia. These problems may be consistent with a familial pattern of neurodevelopmental disability.

In contrast to his specific deficits in spelling and handwriting resulting in a learning disability involving written expression, Kurt shows superior reading and math skills, is orally articulate, and shows appropriate behavior patterns for his age. It is difficult to establish prognoses for such children; although Kurt's skills in spelling and handwriting are likely to improve, these areas will be uniquely difficult for him. The following suggestions were offered to Kurt's parents and school personnel:

1. Because handwriting is an extremely difficult task that practice is not likely to enhance, Kurt's knowledge of subject matter could be assessed better using methods requiring limited production of written language (e.g., a multiple-choice response format is preferable to short answer).

2. To encourage the development of written language skills, use of dictation, a typewriter, or a word processor is recommended. Dysgraphia is a specific impairment affecting the ability to write or copy language. The *generation* of language, however, does not appear to be affected. Therefore, the use of assistive devices like dictation, or transcription with a typewriter or processor, is strongly advised to encourage the production of written language.

3. Because spelling is likely to be a major impediment for Kurt, spelling techniques that rely on orthographic features of words are recommended (e.g., "clustering" words into common elements such as "word families," common suffixes like -tion, -able, etc.). A personal spelling dictionary may be helpful. It also might help to have someone proofread Kurt's papers or to use a spelling package on a word processing program.

4. Give Kurt a direct, simplified explanation of the nature of his learning disability. He certainly knows what he cannot do, but it is unclear whether he understands his disability is specific, unique, and of neuropsychological origin.

5. As Kurt progresses through the grades his teachers will need to be sensitized to the nature and severity of his disability. Dysgraphia is a rare condition, and unless Kurt's teachers understand its expression, he may be penalized unfairly for his failure to complete written assignments.

6. Career exploration should be conducted by Kurt and his family within the context of his neuropsychological strengths and weaknesses.

CASE STUDY #6

MATHEMATICS REASONING DISORDER.
(Katy, white female, CA 13-4, grade 7)

Background and Observation:

Katy is a petite, fair-skinned young lady with lovely reddish hair. She wears braces and gives the appearance of being younger than her 13 years. She was referred for evaluation because of concern about her academic performance, particularly in math.

Katy's mother indicated she was the product of a normal pregnancy and delivery. Severe allergies to all milk products were identified when Katy was a neonate, and she had a restricted diet as an infant. Additional allergies have since been identified, and recently Katy has been placed under an allergist's care. Katy takes oral medication (two Entex LA tablets daily) and receives weekly shots for her allergies; she also continues on a special diet.

Mrs. E expressed some concern about Katy's ability to communicate with others, especially unfamiliar adults. She described Katy as generally reserved and quiet, but indicated she does open up when she feels comfortable. In some areas Mrs. E feels Katy acts younger than her age, but in others she is very mature. For example, Katy has a regular baby-sitting job 3 days a week after school.

Mr. and Mrs. E both graduated from high school and have pursued additional training. Mrs. E understood that a nephew of hers (Katy's cousin) had difficulty with math, but she knew few of the details. Mrs. E is right-handed; Mr. E is left-handed. Katy writes with her right hand, but reported she can use her left hand as well. Her handwriting has a marked reverse slant.

Katy's teacher described her as generally reserved and quiet in school. She is perceived by her teacher as anxious and worried about making mistakes. Katy does not request teacher assistance and is working far below grade level in all areas except spelling. Math is Katy's most difficult subject and even her basic math skills seem poorly developed according to the teacher. Katy also has difficulty remembering answers for social studies tests, even when she has just reviewed the material with another student. Her teacher has observed that Katy has difficulty making inferences and drawing conclusions, as well.

On the 2 days of this evaluation Katy seemed a sweet, compliant, though somewhat timid young lady. Her physical appearance is more like that of a 9- or 10-year-old girl than a 13-year-old adolescent. In general Katy's performance was characterized by good attention and concentration, although some tentativeness was observed. Katy frequently took a very long time to respond, as though she were afraid of saying or doing the wrong thing. She was encouraged to say she did not know, did not understand, or to ask for further clarification, but she continued this response style throughout the 2 days of evaluation. Such behavior was particularly evident during tasks requiring abstract reasoning and concept formation, as discussed below.

Test Results:

Wechsler Intelligence Scale for Children-Revised (WISC-R)

Verbal	SS	Performance	SS
Information	8	Picture Completion	11
Similarities	7	Picture Arrangement	10
Arithmetic	8	Block Design	7
Vocabulary	8	Object Assembly	(W)5
Comprehension	9	Coding	(S)13
Digit Span	7		

Verbal IQ = 87   Performance IQ = 93

Full Scale IQ = 89

These results suggest that on the average Katy's intellectual ability falls within the low-average range, equivalent to the 23rd percentile of the general population. There is no significant difference between Katy's Verbal and Performance scores, although she exhibits a significant weakness on Object Assembly, a task requiring integration of parts into a whole, and a significant strength on Coding, a task of rapid visual motor speed. Because of high intra-factor variability, no clear information processing patterns were evident from recategorization of the scores according to Bannatyne's model.

Woodcock-Johnson Psychoeducational Battery (WJPB)- Achievement Tests

Cluster	SS	%	GE
Reading	95	36	7.0
Mathematics	80	9	5.3
Written Language	99	48	7.8
Knowledge	88	21	5.6

Based on her intellectual ability score, Katy's achievement is within the average range, at or above predicted levels, in all areas except for math. Her mathematics cluster score is slightly, though not significantly, below her intellectual ability score as measured by the WISC-R. A difference of 9 points between the WISC-R Full Scale IQ and the WJPB mathematics cluster score could occur by chance alone.

Further analysis of individual subtest scores comprising the WJPB mathematics cluster reveals that Katy performed more poorly on the Applied Problems (i.e., math reasoning) subtest than on the Calculation task. Derived scores for the two subtests are as follows:

Subtest	SS	%	GE
Applied Problems	65	1	4.6
Calculation	87	19	7.1

These results suggest that mathematics reasoning is a more significant weakness for Katy than mathematics computation, and that the difference between this score and Katy's intellectual ability approaches a severe discrepancy indicative of a specific learning disability.

Item analysis of Katy's performance on the WJPB math cluster indicates computation errors in addition and several in long division problems, a process she does not appear to understand. Interestingly, Katy did have success on problems requiring addition and subtraction of fractions, a skill that has been rehearsed extensively in recent tutoring sessions.

In the applied problems area, Katy demonstrated lack of understanding of a number of basic mathematics concepts, including place value. She had great difficulty adding monetary values, a skill most children have mastered at a considerably younger age.

Boder Test of Reading/Spelling Patterns

Katy's reading quotient was 107, within the average range. She spelled 70% of known words correctly and 70% of unknown words as good phonic equivalents. Katy's performance is consistent with the test authors' criteria for a normal reading/spelling profile.

Test of Written Language (TOWL)

Selected subtests of the TOWL were administered in order to assess Katy's written expression to a greater extent than provided on the WJPB. Scores were as follows:

Subtest	SS
Vocabulary	12
Thematic Maturity	11
Thought Units	11
Handwriting	8

These results suggest that Katy's written expression is within normal limits for her age. Examination of her creative writing selection demonstrated good quantity and fair quality of production.

Aphasia Screening Test

Katy's performance on the AST was within normal limits, demonstrating no pathognomonic signs of language-related learning disabilities.

Halstead Category Test

Katy made 54 errors on the Category Test, which is a moderately impaired performance for her age. The score alone does not reflect the extreme difficulty Katy experienced on this task. She required extraordinary amounts of examiner assistance to proceed on the task, and often needed a great deal of urging and encouragement to select an answer. She had great difficulty forming, testing, and modifying hypotheses. Because these are the types of cognitive processes involved in mathematics reasoning tasks, it is likely Katy's weakness in concept formation is related to her poor performance in mathematics.

Trail Making Task

Katy's performance is slightly to significantly impaired (Trails A = 28 seconds; Trails B = 42 seconds), providing further evidence of neuropsychological dysfunction.

Finger Oscillation

Although Katy demonstrated the typical degree of difference in tapping speed between the two hands, her tapping speed in general is slightly depressed (RH = 38 taps/10 seconds; LH = 34 taps/10 seconds). This performance provides further evidence of subtle neuropsychological impairment, and particularly implicates the anterior regions. Dysfunction in these areas may be demonstrated in expressive weaknesses and is consistent with Katy's difficulties on the Category Test as well.

Child Behavior Checklist-Parent Edition

Mrs. E completed the CBCL regarding children's behavior problems. According to her responses, Katy's behavior was within normal limits for girls her age.

Child Behavior Checklist-Teacher Edition

Katy's teacher completed the teacher edition of the CBCL. Her ratings indicated that Katy's behavior is not significantly different from her peers', although she exhibits some elevation on internalizing scales (e.g., anxiety, social withdrawal).

Summary and Recommendations:

Katy is a reserved, intense young lady who appears younger than her chronological age of 13 years. She has a history of extensive allergies, for which she is currently under a doctor's care. School officials perceive Katy as timid and shy. They indicate she is reluctant to ask for teacher assistance and is having difficulty in nearly all subject areas.

Current testing indicates that Katy is of low average intellectual ability, with relative weaknesses in subtests sensitive to perceptual organization ability and concept formation. Her achievement test scores are at or above expected levels in all areas except for mathematics, which represents a particular deficit for Katy.

Qualitative interpretation of test results provides additional information that may suggest the presence of a specific learning disability, most significantly on such measures as finger tapping, the Category Test, and the Trail Making Test. In addition, the pattern of strengths and weaknesses on the WISC-R, showing relatively greater difficulty with perceptual organizational tasks, is consistent with a specific learning disability in mathematics. Analysis of Katy's error pattern on the WJPB mathematics cluster reveals major gaps in her knowledge and understanding, suggesting that remediation of key areas will be to her advantage.

These results suggest Katy could benefit from a modified educational program. The following are recommendations:

1. Provide systematic instruction in abstract reasoning and concept formation. Examples of such activities include seeing relationships, categorization, hypothesis testing, and problem solving.
2. Incorporate diagnostic-prescriptive teaching in mathematics. Certain key areas were observed to be outside of Katy's current level of understanding, including the concept of place value, understanding and adding monetary values, and the process of long division. Identification of such weaknesses, with systematic instruction in them, would be to Katy's advantage.
3. Provide a program that is suitably supportive and protective. Katy appears in many ways younger and less sophisticated than the average girl of 13. She has a protective, supportive family, and has attended school in a similar environment. Even within this setting she is perceived as timid and reserved. In determining an appropriate educational placement for Katy, her parents and school officials should consider Katy's temperament and lifestyle, and strive to provide her with adequate support.

REFERENCES

Achenbach, T. M., & Edelbrock, C. (1983). *Manual for the Child Behavior Checklist*. Burlington, VT: University Associates in Psychiatry.

ACLD offers new definition of learning disabilities. (1985). *Special Education Today, 2*, pp. 1, 19.

American Psychiatric Association. (1980). *Diagnostic and Statistical Manual of Mental Disorders* (3rd ed.). Washington, DC: Author.

Aram, D. M., Ekelman, B. L., Rose, D. F., & Whitaker, H. A. (1985). Verbal and cognitive sequelae following unilateral lesions acquired in early childhood. *Journal of Clinical and Experimental Neuropsychology, 7*, 55-78.

Bakan, P., Dibb, G., & Reed, P. (1973). Handedness and birth stress. *Neuropsychologia, 11*, 363-366.

Bannatyne, A. (1974). A note on recategorization of the WISC scaled scores. *Journal of Learning Disabilities, 7*, 272-274.

Bannatyne, A. (1978). The spatially competent LD child. *Academic Therapy, 14*, 133-155.

Beery, K. E. (1982). *Revised Administration, Scoring, and Teaching Manual for the Developmental Test of Visual-Motor Integration*. Chicago: Follett Publishing Co.

Benton, A. L., Hamsher, K. deS., Varney, N. R., & Spreen, O. (1983). *Contributions to Neuropsychological Assessment*. New York: Oxford University Press.

Boder, E. (1973). Developmental dyslexia: A diagnostic approach based on three atypical reading-spelling patterns. *Developmental Medicine and Child Neurology, 15*, 663-687.

Boder, E., & Jarrico, S. (1982). *The Boder Test of Reading-Spelling Patterns, Manual*. New York: Grune & Stratton.

Boll, T. J., & Reitan, R. M. (1972). Motor and tactile-perceptual deficits in brain damaged children. *Perceptual and Motor Skills, 34*, 343-350.

Bolter, J. F., & Long, C. J. (1985). Methodological issues in research in developmental neuropsychology. In L. C. Hartlage & C. F. Telzrow (Eds.), *The Neuropsychology of Individual Differences: A Developmental Perspective* (pp. 41-59). New York: Plenum.

Brown, R. T., & Alford, N. (1984). Ameliorating attentional deficits and concomitant academic deficiencies in learning disabled children through cognitive training. *Journal of Learning Disabilities, 17,* 20-26.

Cermak, L. S. (1983). Information processing deficits in children with learning disabilities. *Journal of Learning Disabilities, 16,* 599-605.

Connors, C. (1969). A teacher rating scale for use in drug studies with children. *American Journal of Psychiatry, 126,* 884-888.

Connors, C. K. (1982). Parent and teacher rating forms for the assessment of hyperkinesis in children. In P. A. Keller & L. G. Ritt (Eds.), *Innovations in Clinical Practice: A Source Book* (Vol. 1, pp. 257-264). Sarasota, FL: Professional Resource Exchange, Inc.

Coolidge, F. L., Bracken, D. D., Andrews, L. W., & Pennington, B. F. (1985). Cross-validation of the Selz-Reitan pattern index. *The International Journal of Clinical Neuropsychology, 7,* 122-123.

Cronbach, L. J., & Snow, R. E. (1977). *Aptitudes and Instructional Methods.* New York: Irvington Publishers, Inc.

Dean, R. S. (1982). Neuropsychological assessment. In T. Kratochwill (Ed.), *Advances in School Psychology* (Vol. 2, pp. 171-201). New Jersey: Lawrence Erlbaum.

Dean, R. S. (1986) Perspectives on the future of neuropsychological assessment. In B. S. Plake & J. C. Witt (Eds.), *Buros-Nebraska Series on Measurement and Testing: Future of Testing and Measurement* (pp. 203-244). New Jersey: Lawrence Erlbaum.

DeFilippis, N., & McCampbell, E. (1979). *The Booklet Category Test.* Odessa, FL: Psychological Assessment Resources, Inc.

Denckla, M. B., LeMay, M., & Chapman, C. A. (1985). Few CT scan abnormalities found even in neurologically impaired learning disabled children. *Journal of Learning Disabilities, 18,* 132-135.

Dorman, C. (1982). Personality and psychiatric correlates of the Halstead-Reitan tests in boys with school problems. *Clinical Neuropsychology, 4,* 110-114.

Douglas, V. I. (1983). Attentional and cognitive problems. In M. Rutter (Ed.), *Developmental Neuropsychiatry* (pp. 280-329). New York: The Guilford Press.

Federally funded study shows imagery boosts learning, recall. (1984, December). *Brain/Mind Bulletin,* p. 3.

Finlayson, M. A. J., & Reitan, R. M. (1976). Handedness in relation to measures of motor and tactile perceptual functions in normal children. *Perceptual and Motor Skills, 43,* 475-481.

Flavell, J. H. (1977). *Cognitive Development.* Englewood Cliffs, NJ: Prentice-Hall, Inc.

Gaddes, W. H. (1983). Applied educational neuropsychology: Theories and problems. *Journal of Learning Disabilities, 16,* 511-514.

Galaburda, A. (1983). Developmental dyslexia: Current anatomical research. *Annals of Dyslexia, 33,* 41-53.

Galaburda, A. M., & Kemper, T. L. (1979). Cytoarchitectonic abnormalities in developmental dyslexia: A case study. *Annals of Neurology, 6,* 94-100.

Geschwind, N. (1979). Specializations of the human brain. In *The Brain* (pp. 108-117). San Francisco: W. H. Freeman & Co.

Geschwind, N., & Behan, P. (1982). Left-handedness: Association with immune disease, migraine, and developmental learning disorders. *Proceedings of the National Academy of Science, 79,* 5097-5100.

Geschwind, N., & Levitsky, W. (1968). Human brain, left-right asymmetries in temporal speech region. *Science, 161,* 186-187.

Gesell, A., Halverson, H. M., Thompson, H., Ilg, F. L., Costner, B. M., Ames, L. B., & Amatruda, C. S. (1940). *The First Five Years of Life: A Guide to the Study of the Preschool Child.* New York: Harper & Row.

Golden, C. J., & Sawicki, R. F. (1985). Neuropsychological bases of psychopathological disorders. In L. C. Hartlage & C. F. Telzrow (Eds.), *The Neuropsychology of Individual Differences: A Developmental Perspective* (pp. 203-236). New York: Plenum.

Gottfried, A. W., & Bathurst, K. (1983). Hand preference across time is related to intelligence in young girls, not boys. *Science, 221,* 1074-1076.

Gutkin, T. B., & Reynolds, C. R. (1981). Examination of the Selz and Reitan scatter index of neurological dysfunction with a nationally representative sample of normal children. *Clinical Neuropsychology, 3,* 38-41.

Hallahan, D. P., & Sapona, R. (1983). Self-monitoring of attention with learning-disabled children: Past research and current issues. *Journal of Learning Disabilities, 16,* 616-620.

Hartlage, L. C., & Telzrow, C. F. (1982). Neuropsychological assessment. In K. Paget & B. Bracken (Eds.), *Psychoeducational Assessment of Preschool and*

Primary Aged Children (pp. 295-320). New York: Grune & Stratton. (a)

Hartlage, L. C., & Telzrow, C. F. (1982). Specific medical tests which predict specific learning outcomes. In W. Cruickshank & J. Lerner (Eds.), *Coming of Age* (Vol. 3, the best of ACLD, pp. 36-44). Syracuse, NY: Syracuse University Press. (b)

Hartlage, L. C., & Telzrow, C. F. (1983). The neuropsychological bases of educational intervention. *Journal of Learning Disabilities, 16,* 521-528.

Hartlage, L. C., & Telzrow, C. F. (1985). Neuropsychological aspects of educational intervention. *Information/Edge: Neuropsychology and Special Education, 1*(2), 1, 4.

Henry, S. A., & Wittman, R. D. (1981). Diagnostic implications of Bannatyne's recategorized WISC-R scores for identifying learning disabled children. *Journal of Learning Disabilities, 14,* 517-520.

Hessler, G. L. (1982). *Use and Interpretation of the Woodcock-Johnson Psycho-Educational Battery.* Hingham, MA: Teaching Resources Corp.

Jorm, A. F. (1983). Specific reading retardation and working memory: A review. *British Journal of Psychology, 74,* 311-342.

Kaufman, A. S. (1979). *Intelligent Testing with the WISC-R.* New York: John Wiley & Sons.

Kaufman, A. S. (1981). The WISC-R and learning disabilities assessment: State of the art. *Journal of Learning Disabilities, 14,* 520-526.

Kaufman, A. S., Zalma, R., & Kaufman, N. L. (1978). Motor coordination, mental ability, and right-left awareness of young normal children. *Child Development, 49,* 885-888.

Kavale, K. (1982). The efficacy of stimulant drug treatment for hyperactivity: A meta-analysis. *Journal of Learning Disabilities, 15,* 280-289.

Knights, R. M., & Moule, A. D. (1968). Normative data on the motor steadiness battery for children. *Perceptual and Motor Skills, 26,* 643-650.

Knights, R. M., & Norwood, J. A. (1980). *Revised Smooth Normative Data on the Neuropsychological Test Battery for Children.* Ottawa, CA: Department of Psychology.

Knights, R. M., & Norwood, J. A. (undated). *A Neuropsychological Test Battery for Children: Examiner's Manual.* Ottawa, Canada: Psychological Consultants, Inc.

Levy, J. (1985). Right brain, left brain: Fact and fiction. *Psychology Today, 19*(5), 38-44.

Luria, A. R. (1966). *Higher Cortical Functions in Man.* New York: Basic Books.

Malloy, P. F., Webster, J. S., & Russell, W. (1985). Tests of Luria's frontal lobe syndromes. *International Journal of Clinical Neuropsychology, 7,* 88-95.

Marston, D., & Ysseldyke, J. (1980). *Derived Subtest Scores for the Woodcock-Johnson Psycho-Educational Battery.* Hingham, MA: Teaching Resources Corp.

McCauley, C., & Ciesielski, J. (1982). Electro-encephalogram tests for brain dysfunction: A question of validity. *Science, 217,* 81-82.

McKay, S., Stelling, M. W., Bauman, R. J., Carr, W. A., Walsh, J. W., & Gilmore, R. L. (1985). Assessment of frontal lobe dysfunction using the Luria-Nebraska Neuropsychological Battery-Children's Revision: A case study. *International Journal of Clinical Neuropsychology, 7,* 107-111.

Mercer, J. R., & Lewis, J. F. (1978). *System of Multicultural Pluralistic Assessment.* New York: The Psychological Corp.

Nocera, S. D. (1979). *Reaching the Special Learner through Music.* Morristown, NJ: Silver Burdett Co.

Nockleby, D. M., & Galbraith, G. G. (1984). Developmental dyslexia subtypes and the Boder Test of Reading-Spelling Patterns. *Journal of Psychoeducational Assessment, 2,* 91-100.

Palmer, H., & Palmer, P. (1971). *Singing Multiplication Tables* (Record). Freeport, NY: Educational Activities, Inc.

Piaget, J. (1975). The stages of intellectual development of the child. In H. Munsinger (Ed.), *Readings in Child Development* (2nd ed., pp. 124-130). New York: Holt, Rinehart, & Winston.

Pirozzolo, F. J. (1979). *The Neuropsychology of Developmental Reading Disorders.* New York: Praeger Publishers.

Reeve, R. E., Hall, R. J., & Zakreski, R. S. (1979). The Woodcock-Johnson Tests of Cognitive Ability: Concurrent validity with the WISC-R. *Learning Disability Quarterly, 2,* 63-69.

Reitan, R. M. (1971). Trail Making Test results for normal and brain-damaged children. *Perceptual and Motor Skills, 33,* 571-581.

Reitan, R. M. (1979). *Manual for Administration of Neuropsychological Test Batteries for Adults and Children.* Tucson, AZ: Reitan Neuropsychology Laboratories, Inc.

Reynolds, C. R. (1984). Psychometric characteristics of the Boder Test of Reading-Spelling Patterns. *School Psychology Review, 13,* 526-529.

Rourke, B. P., & Finlayson, M. A. J. (1978). Neuropsychological significance of variations in patterns of academic performance: Verbal and visual-spatial abilities. *Journal of Abnormal Child Psychology, 6,* 121-133.

Rourke, B. P., & Strang, J. D. (1983). Subtypes of reading and arithmetical disabilities: A neuropsychological analysis. In M. Rutter (Ed.), *Developmental Neuropsychiatry* (pp. 473-488). New York: The Guilford Press.

Rugel, R. (1974). WISC subtest scores of disabled readers: A review with respect to Bannatyne's recategorization. *Journal of Learning Disabilities, 7,* 48-55.

Sattler, J. M. (1982). *Assessment of Children's Intelligence and Special Abilities.* Boston: Allyn & Bacon.

Selz, M. (1981). Halstead-Reitan Neuropsychological Test Batteries for children. In G. W. Hynd & J. E. Obrzut (Eds.), *Neuropsychological Assessment and the School-Age Child* (pp. 195-235). New York: Grune & Stratton.

Selz, M., & Reitan, R. M. (1979). Rules for neuropsychological diagnosis: Classification of brain function in older children. *Journal of Consulting and Clinical Psychology, 47,* 258-264.

Sparrow, S. S., Balla, D. A., & Cicchetti, D. V. (1984). *Vineland Adaptive Behavior Scales.* Circle Pines, MN: American Guidance Services.

Taylor, H. G., Fletcher, J. M., & Satz, P. (1984). Neuropsychological assessment of children. In G. Goldstein & M. Hersen (Eds.), *Handbook of Psychological Assessment* (pp. 211-234). New York: Pergamon Press.

Telzrow, C. F., Century, E., Redmond, C., Whitaker, B., & Zimmerman, B. (1983). The Boder Test: Neuropsychological and demographic features of dyslexic subtypes. *Psychology in the Schools, 20,* 427-432.

Telzrow, C. F., & Hartlage, L. C. (1983). Evaluation and programming for infants and preschoolers with neurological and neuropsychological impairments. In C. R. Reynolds & J. H. Clark (Eds.), *Assessment and*

Programming for Children with Low-Incidence Handicaps (pp. 43-118). New York: Plenum.

Telzrow, C. F., & Speer, B. (in press). Learning disabled children: General suggestions for maximizing instruction. *Techniques.* (a)

Telzrow, C. F., & Speer, B. (in press). Neuropsychologically based learning disorders: Implications for instruction. *Techniques.* (b)

Thornton, C., & Noxon, C. (1977). *Look into the Facts.* Palo Alto, CA: Creative Publications, Inc.

Torgesen, J. K. (1982). The study of short-term memory in learning disabled children: Goals, methods, and conclusions. In K. D. Gadow & I. Bialer (Eds.), *Advances in Learning and Behavioral Disabilities* (pp. 117-149). Greenwich, CT: JAI Press.

Tsai, L. Y. (1982). Handedness in autistic children and their families. *Journal of Autism and Developmental Disorders, 12,* 421-423.

Werner, E. E., Honzik, M. P., & Smith, R. S. (1968). Prediction of intelligence and achievement at 10 years from 21 months pediatric and psychologic examinations. *Child Development, 30,* 1063-1075.

Ysseldyke, J., Shinn, M., & Epps, S. (1981). A comparison of the WISC-R and the Woodcock-Johnson Tests of Cognitive Ability. *Psychology in the Schools, 18,* 15-19.

Zingale, S. A., & Smith, M. D. (1978). WISC-R patterns for learning disabled children at three SES levels. *Psychology in the Schools, 15,* 199-204.

4

SPECIAL CONSIDERATIONS REGARDING THE ASSESSMENT OF PRESCHOOL CHILDREN

INTRODUCTION

The assessment of preschool youngsters introduces some special problems requiring a somewhat different approach to evaluation. Both the types of questions to be answered and the means of answering them are unique for this population. In addition to the obviously restricted sample of measurable behaviors available in preschoolers, the influence of developmental variability introduced in Chapter 3 is especially critical for very young children. Neuropsychological disorders frequently are displayed on available measures as diffuse rather than discrete conditions, which complicates questions related to diagnosis, individual program planning, and prognosis. Neurological impairment, even when documented by hard medical evidence, is highly variable in its expression from one age to another. Even a neat, localized lesion in the left or right hemisphere may not result in the expected lateralized findings when it occurs very early (K. B. Fitzhugh, L. C. Fitzhugh, & Reitan, 1962).

Despite these assessment limitations, early identification of developmental problems is extremely important. Intervention with children during the preschool period results in greater success for these individuals (Lazar & Darlington, 1978; Schweinhart & Weikart, 1980); even the difference between intervention initiated at age 2 versus 3 years for children with impaired hearing has significant impact on subsequent language skills (Horton, 1974). Such findings suggest that although the assessment of preschool children is fraught with special kinds of problems, the resulting benefits for children and their families make such efforts worthwhile.

This chapter reviews the assessment process for preschool children. In cases where the procedures are similar to those described for older youngsters in the preceding chapter, only brief references are made to those previously described activities, and where unique procedures or techniques are relevant for the preschool population, a more thorough discussion is provided.

PRE-EVALUATION ACTIVITIES

As with older children, a pre-evaluation interview with the parent(s) is recommended to collect valuable background information and help establish preliminary hypotheses about observed symptomatology, which is pursued later during individual assessment. Empathy and sensitivity are especially critical when interacting with parents of preschool children because this may be the first time a question has been raised about the child's development. Parents who have a handicapped child experience stages of grieving similar to those encountered at the death of a son or daughter (Drotar, Baskiewicz, Irving, Kennell, & Klaus, 1975; Moses, 1984), and early coping mechanisms such as anger or denial require special sensitivity on the part of the clinician.

MEDICAL HISTORY

As with older children, a comprehensive health history is critical to a complete neuropsychological assessment. Its importance for young children is compounded by the relatively short time period these youngsters have had to recover from major medical traumas, as well as the often devastating effects on normal development from such infant episodes as seizures, infections, or head injury (L. C. Hartlage, Stovall, & P. L. Hartlage, 1980; Klonoff, Low, & Clark, 1977). The interview procedure and the content areas described in the third chapter apply for younger children as well.

DEVELOPMENTAL HISTORY

In addition to determining the child's mastery of developmental milestones, comparison of language and nonlanguage milestones must be conducted. We have reported age-appropriate language and nonlanguage activities at half-year intervals from ages 2 to 6 years (Telzrow & L. C. Hartlage, 1983). By evaluating whether or not the child has attained the skills appropriate for his or her chronological age, the clinician can make some assumptions about general developmental level. In addition, if the pattern of skill mastery suggests a consistent weakness in either language or nonlanguage abilities, an hypothesis about a specific profile of neuropsychological strengths and weaknesses is suggested, to be investigated further by direct assessment.

A general question frequently asked of parents of preschool children during the developmental interview is, "All in all, how old a child does Sam seem to you?" In our experience, supported by research evidence (Coplan, 1982; Evans & Sparrow, 1976), parents have an uncanny ability to identify the child's developmental level correctly, even though they may not have accepted cognitively that the child has significant delays. Recently, for example, the second author evaluated a severely retarded 3-1/2-year-old child whose uneducated mother had expressed great anxiety and distress about being told her child was mentally retarded. And yet despite her fears, when asked to estimate her son's functioning level, she stated without hesitation, "About 1 year," an estimate quite consistent with all other data.

In addition to the parent interview regarding developmental history, we typically incorporate at least one formal developmental inventory with the parent as informant. Any of the parent-report measures listed in Table 2 (pp. 114-115) may be appropriate, depending upon the age of the youngster and the sophistication level of the caregiver. We prefer the Minnesota Child Development Inventory (MCDI) and the Vineland Adaptive Behavior Scale (VABS). The former is a 320-item forced choice (yes-no) scale designed to be completed by the parent. Developmental age scores are reported for seven domains, as well as a total score. The VABS uses an interview format, and hence may be preferred in situations where the reading level of the parent may present a limitation. The VABS reports standard scores,

TABLE 2: COMMON INSTRUMENTS USED IN ASSESSMENT OF NEUROPSYCHOLOGICAL DISORDERS IN PRESCHOOL CHILDREN

Category	Possible Instruments	Publisher
Cognitive Ability	1. Bayley Scales of Infant Development	The Psychological Corporation
	2. McCarthy Scales of Children's Abilities (MSCA)	The Psychological Corporation
	3. Kaufman Assessment Battery for Children (K-ABC)	American Guidance Services
	4. Leiter International Performance Scale	Stoelting Publishing Company
	5. Woodcock-Johnson Psychoeducational Battery (WJPB) - Cognitive Scale	DLM-Teaching Resources
	6. Stanford-Binet Intelligence Scale	Riverside Publishing Company
	7. Wechsler Preschool and Primary Scale of Intelligence (WPPSI)	The Psychological Corporation
Basic Language Skills	1. Receptive - Expressive Emergent Language Scale (REEL)	University Park Press
	2. Language Sample of 50 Utterances	See Dale, 1976
	3. Preschool Language Scale (PLS)	Charles Merrill
	4. Clinical Evaluation of Language Functions (CELF)	Charles Merrill
	5. Peabody Picture Vocabulary Test - Revised (PPVT-R)	American Guidance Services
	6. Expressive One Word Picture Vocabulary Test	American Therapy Publications
	7. K-ABC Achievement	American Guidance Services
	8. Test of Early Language Development (TELD)	PRO-ED
	9. Token Test for Children	DLM-Teaching Resources
	10. Test for Auditory Comprehension of Language (TACL)	DLM-Teaching Resources
Pre-Academic Skills	1. K-ABC Achievement	American Guidance Services
	2. WJPB Achievement	DLM-Teaching Resources

Category	Possible Instruments	Publisher
Motor Ability	1. Bayley Scales of Infant Development 2. Developmental Test of Visual Motor Integration (Beery VMI) 3. Motor Domains on Developmental Inventories (See Below)	The Psychological Corporation Follett Publishing Company See Individual Scales
Sensory Ability	1. Motor Free Visual Perception Test 2. Sensory - Perceptual Tasks	Academic Therapy Publications See Benton, Hamsher, Varney, and Spreen, 1983; Knights and Norwood, undated, 1980; Reitan, 1979
Social Behavior	1. Carey Infant Temperament Scale 2. Child Behavior Checklist 3. California Preschool Social Competency Scale	Author University Associates in Psychiatry Consulting Psychologists Press
Self-Care Skills	1. Vineland Adaptive Behavior Scale 2. Self-Care Domains on Development Inventories (See Below)	American Guidance Services See Individual Scales
Developmental Inventories	1. Vineland Adaptive Behavior Scale 2. Minnesota Child Development Inventory (MCDI) 3. Developmental Profile II 4. Battelle Developmental Inventory (BDI)	American Guidance Services Behavior Science Systems Psychological Developmental Publications DLM-Teaching Resources

percentiles, and age scores for four domains (daily living skills, communication, socialization, and motor), with subdomain scores also available.

In addition to the obvious advantage of having a profile of scores from a formal developmental inventory, which frequently reflects neuropsychological patterns of strengths and weaknesses to be investigated further, use of a parent report scale also establishes an important level of credibility about other assessment data. It is our experience that the data from these scales tend to be very consistent with results from other sources, such as direct assessment of the child. When summarizing results for parents, it is often helpful to begin with the results of the parent report scale, thereby establishing a certain level of acceptance for other supporting data as well.

EDUCATIONAL AND FAMILY HISTORY

The purpose and procedures for collecting information about the educational and family history are similar to those described for older children, with one additional comment. "Educational history," in this context, is interpreted loosely to mean any of a wide variety of educationally relevant experiences, either within or outside the home. Examples of such experiences include nursery school, day care, and formal speech therapy. This information is critical not only because of the obvious relationship between early stimulation and eventual school adjustment, but because of the effects of such experiences (or, more significantly, lack of them) on any direct assessment conducted with the child. For example, exposing children to test-like tasks significantly improves performance (Dreisbach & Keogh, 1982). Similarly, in our experience young children who have had speech therapy are skilled test-takers because they have learned to sit quietly at a table and interact with an adult in a give-and-take manner.

MEASURABLE ABILITIES AND APPROPRIATE INSTRUMENTS AND PROCEDURES

ASSESSMENT PROCEDURES

Unlike the school-aged youngster, for whom most direct assessment can be conducted in a structured test setting, evaluation of preschoolers requires a somewhat more flexible approach and frequently must incorporate several administrative formats. This section begins with an overview of the major ways we use to gather a comprehensive picture of a preschool child. We usually include all sources of information in an evaluation of a youngster because this provides the most complete summary of typical performance levels.

Observation. Observation is listed first as an assessment process because of its recognized value in collecting valid information about young children. Although the cooperation of preschoolers in a structured test situation is frequently difficult to obtain, it is generally possible to gather critical information about the youngster during a systematic observation in a familiar environment. The goals of observation are two-fold: (a) to identify any physical stigmata (e.g., minor anomalies) or gait disturbances that may suggest central nervous system dysfunction; and (b) to evaluate a wide variety of age-appropriate skills relative to play, activities of daily living, communication, and social interaction that may indicate delay or dysfunction. Each of these objectives will be discussed in greater detail below.

Physical Observation. One of the most important outcomes of physical examination of preschool children relates to the identification of minor physical anomalies indicative of underlying central nervous system involvement. Several such physical variations in children's features have been identified, such as those involving the hair (hair whorls; fine, "electric" hair), eyes (epicanthal folds, hypertelorism), mouth (high, steepled, arched palate; furrowed tongue), ears (low-set or asymmetrical ears), hands (single palmar crease, curved fifth digit), and feet (large gap between great toe and other toes, middle toe longest of the five, syndactyly). The expression of these dysmorphic features presumably is caused by some disruption of the intra-uterine environment during the prenatal development of these particular skinfolds. These physical anomalies are significant in the neuropsychological assessment of children because such characteristics have been associated with a variety of subsequent school-related problems, including somewhat lower IQ, hyperactivity, and a tendency to be retained in the early grades (Rosenberg & Weller, 1973; Waldrop & Halverson, 1971; Waldrop, Pederson, & Bell, 1968). These physical stigmata appear to reflect subtle neurologic impairment of brain structures critical for attention, concentration, and school success. This is especially true if they occur in the context of other anomalies and there is evidence of adjustment problems.

A physical observation also may reveal disturbances of motor or sensory systems, to be pursued further during more formal evaluation. Observation of this nature requires that the clinician be extremely familiar with the range of normal physical development milestones for preschoolers of various ages. Such an observation might be conducted in a therapy room or gym in a school or clinic setting, or in the child's home, where he or she can be observed interacting with various types of large and small motor equipment such as balls, blocks, pull toys, and tricycles. With the cooperation of the parent, it is generally possible to observe the child in a variety of motor activities that have developmental significance, such as rising from a supine position (does the child roll onto the tummy or turn to the side in rising?) and maneuvering up and down stairs. Weakness of the hands and fingers might be identified in a child who cannot fasten snaps or put together Lego blocks. Through these observations the clinician may develop hypotheses about the child's motor and sensory development, to be followed up during more formal assessment.

Interactive Observation. This portion of the observation is ideally conducted in an environment familiar to the child, such as the home or preschool setting. If circumstances necessitate conducting the interactive observation in a school or clinic, it is most helpful to provide a nursery school-like setting with a variety of age-appropriate toys, and to have one or both parents present.

The goals of the interactive observation are to identify any atypical behaviors in the child's play, communication skills, activities of daily living, and socialization that might warrant further exploration. The format is highly flexible and varies from child to child, depending on the behaviors observed. The following two examples illustrate what kinds of behaviors might be significant and how the observation might progress.

James, age 2-1/2, is visited at his home. When the examiner enters, the boy is pressed against the door chimes, located in the hallway, which were rung by the examiner a moment earlier. James makes no eye contact with the examiner and seems unaware of her presence. He is ambulatory and has no apparent motor delays. James occasionally dashes unexpectedly from one room to another, sometimes stopping abruptly, and plants his feet firmly to rock back and forth in place. Frequently he goes to the door chimes and strikes them repetitively to hear the sound. Such behavior appears to be compulsive, and his mother generally must intervene in order for him to leave the chimes. Sometimes James crawls about on the floor, picking up small bits of dirt and crumbs and putting them in his mouth. When presented with a variety of toys (ball, telephone, doll, etc.), James treats them all the same - banging them briefly on the table and then discarding them. Occasionally, without apparent reason, James begins to scream and cry, stopping as quickly as he started. No other vocalization is heard. No positive affect (e.g., surprise, delight) is observed at any time. James does not respond to any verbal directions, and does not gesture or initiate any nonverbal communication with either the examiner or his mother.

Alex is a 3-year-old youngster observed in the play area in a clinic setting. His mother and father are with him. Alex looks at the examiner when she approaches, smiles, wide-eyed, and moves slightly behind his mother's chair, peeking out from the side. He carries a He-Man figure that he plays with purposefully, "walking" it along the armchair and "jumping" it onto his mother's lap. When presented with a variety of toys (e.g., ball, telephone, truck), Alex plays with each in an appropriate manner. He and his father toss a ball back and forth from a distance of about 4 or 5 feet, and Alex smiles shyly at the examiner's enthusiasm. He completes a five-piece puzzle and stacks blocks into a three-dimensional "bridge." Alex places the telephone to his ear and jabbers expressively; he is heard to say "bye" just before he hangs up the phone. Alex occasionally approaches one of the adults in the room and gestures to them, once raising his foot and pointing to his untied shoe. Often he babbles in a kind of jargon with considerable inflection, but no discernible language is heard. Alex responds to a few simple words or commands, such as turning to the sound of his name and showing his shoe on request.

These anecdotes portray two unique preschoolers. Although both James and Alex demonstrate atypical behavior, the nature of the impairment suggested by their behavior differs considerably. Both boys exhibited significant delays in receptive and expressive language. However, James displayed no communicative intent, whereas Alex demonstrated an interest in interacting with others, as judged by his eye contact and nonverbal communication in approaching and gesturing to others. Alex exhibited much normal toy play and had appropriate gestural communication (e.g., placing telephone to his ear). James, on the other hand, showed no curiosity about the examiner's toys, and treated each in the same stereotypic manner. The affect of the two boys was markedly different: Alex reflected typical reactions, such as shyness, curiosity, and pleasure, whereas James responded to all events with a pronounced dull affect. Both boys appeared to have normal motor development, although Alex additionally exhibited age-appropriate cognitive skills on nonlanguage tasks (e.g., block building, puzzle solving). Alex demonstrated none of the bizarre behaviors so characteristic of James (e.g., fixation on nonlinguistic sounds, picking up and eating bits of dust from the floor).

The hypotheses established about these two youngsters during the interactive observation subsequently were confirmed. James is a youngster with an atypical developmental syndrome best identified as childhood autism. The pervasive level of mental retardation, together with lack of appropriate toy play, failure to demonstrate any communicative intent, lack of positive affect, and bizarre behaviors are often characteristic of this condition. Alex displayed a significant language disorder subsequently identified as verbal auditory agnosia, a disruption of the phonologic decoding of language. Despite his significant language disturbance, James displayed much communicative intent. His toy play was age appropriate, as was his gestural communication. Finally, the demonstration of success on age-appropriate cognitive tasks of a nonverbal nature argues against a general intellectual delay and suggests the presence of a specific language disorder.

Parent/Teacher Report Scales. It is often not possible to obtain a good measure of a young child's *typical* performance during a structured evaluation. As a result, we frequently incorporate a parent or teacher report scale as part of a comprehensive assessment of preschool children. An additional benefit of a parent report measure, as mentioned earlier, is that the results of this device can serve as an important credibility anchor when discussing test findings with parents.

Standardized Testing. Use of standardized instruments in a structured administrative format is certainly a procedure we advocate, although we very rarely base a complete evaluation on this alone. Direct assessment of a child in a standardized manner is a means of determining several things, including whether or not the child accommodates to structure, and what his or her ability is to follow directions, to inhibit impulsivity appropriately, and to wait when necessary. It also provides an index of the child's flexibility and how the youngster copes with mild frustration. Finally, a standardized setting is an excellent test of the child's stamina and to what degree he or she is ready for a school-like environment.

Clinicians whose experience generally has been limited to school-aged children must be cautioned, however, that standardized testing of preschoolers requires a bit more than a smaller table and chair! The behavior of a 2-year-old may be *typically* resistant and capricious. We interpret such behaviors as a reflection of normalcy rather than of any pathological significance, as they might be in older children. The major key to success in direct assessment of preschoolers, we have found, is flexibility. Using this as our watchword, we have not yet encountered an "untestable" child. If a child refuses a task, we introduce a different one, or, on occasion, move to a chat with the parent and attempt the task again when the child's curiosity has been aroused. If the 3-year-old cannot manage on the K-ABC or the McCarthy, we back up to a measure such as the Bayley. We sometimes employ concrete rewards, though we find this is necessary with only a small minority of children. Clearly, these examples imply a substantial commitment of time on the part of the examiner because it often is not possible to complete the assessment measures and strategies that had been intended if the youngster is fearful, resistant, or distractible. The examiner should, of course, expect such behavior when assessing preschool children. Almost always, in our experience, failure to obtain some response from the child should be attributed to the examiner and not to the youngster.

MEASURABLE ABILITIES
AND POSSIBLE INSTRUMENTS

Cognitive. The purposes of cognitive assessment in preschool children are similar to those described previously for older youngsters: to determine general intellectual level and to identify intra-individual variability that may indicate neuropsychological impairment. The formal measures of cognitive ability listed in Table 2 are those utilized by the authors to assess young children. Often two or more of these instruments are used together to further delineate information processing strengths and weaknesses. The first case study at the conclusion of this chapter illustrates how scores derived from a combination of cognitive measures can provide important diagnostic information.

For very young or delayed children (i.e., developmental levels under 2-1/2 years), our preferred measure is the Bayley Scales of Infant Abilities. The main scores derived from this instrument (mental development index and motor development index) unfortunately are not helpful for analyzing individual strengths and weaknesses. However, a supplemental scoring system, called the Kent Scale or Kent Scoring Adaptation for the Bayley (Reuter, Stancin, & Craig, 1981), has been developed that facilitates such intra-individual comparisons. The Kent Scale clusters the Bayley items into five domains - cognitive, social, language, gross motor, and fine motor - for which developmental age scores can be derived. It is a valuable supplement to interpretation of the Bayley performance.

Similar disadvantages exist with the current Binet scale, which reports only mental age and IQ scores. Sattler's (1982) "Binetgram" provides a systematic procedure for analyzing a child's performance to identify individual patterns of strengths and weaknesses. The recently published fourth edition of the Binet derives separate scores for a variety of neuropsychologically relevant processes, including verbal, spatial, and memory abilities. This revision promises to be a more valuable tool than its predecessor in the identification of intra-individual variability.

Basic Language Skills. Because language is such an identifiable behavioral trait in very young children, its presence or absence is often used by adults as a barometer of overall development. Verbally fluent preschoolers are often described as "very bright" though their intellectual levels may be average. Similarly, it is our experience that in children whose language milestones are delayed, for whatever reason (general mental retardation, specific language delay, cerebral palsy), the absence of speech is identified as the area of concern. Hence a parent's report that the child "doesn't talk good" may be a sign of generalized delay or an indication of a specific language disorder.

As with older children, assessment of basic language skills in preschoolers includes an appraisal of both language understanding and use. As mentioned earlier, a single instrument that reports scores for both areas is generally preferred, because of psychometric problems that arise when attempting to equate scores from separate tests. Table 2 lists a number of tools appropriate for the assessment of basic language skills in preschoolers.

Two of the measures included in Table 2 utilize a slightly different administrative format. The first of these, the Receptive-Expressive Emergent Language Scale (REEL), uses a parent or caregiver as informant. It is generally used with infants or older children who exhibit extreme delays in the development of language skills. It is quite helpful for assessing the degree to which a nonverbal child demonstrates communicative intent, which can be important for the differential diagnosis of a specific language disorder and childhood autism.

The second procedure that employs an atypical administrative format is the language sample. Most speech pathologists agree that analysis of a language sample of 50 or so of the child's utterances provides one of the more useful measures of expressive speech. However, because this procedure requires some tenacity on the part of the clinician and is sometimes tedious to analyze, it is not routinely used as a preferred measure of expressive speech. We find that one of the easiest ways to collect a sample of 50 utterances is to tape record the interactive observation and the formal assessment. A simple measure of expressive speech that can be derived from analysis of this sample is the *mean length of utterance*, or MLU. The MLU simply refers to the average length of the child's utterances in morphemes: an MLU of 3 means that, on the average, the child combines three morphemes (e.g., "John go home," "Me eat ice cream"). As a rule of thumb, an MLU that matches the chronological age of the child is considered within normal limits (e.g., a 3-year-old would be expected to have an MLU of 3). In addition to this rather gross index of the quality of expressive speech, the language sample can be analyzed to provide a measure of the child's vocabulary, syntax, and other qualitative indicators of expressive speech. For additional information regarding analysis of a language sample, readers are referred to Dale (1976).

Pre-Academic Skills. Formal assessment of achievement is not generally viable for preschool children. However, it is often possible to evaluate pre-academic skills in reading and math, especially for children above age 3. Table 2 lists standardized instruments available for this purpose. We particularly favor the K-ABC, portions of which are appropriate for children as young as 2-1/2.

More informal assessment of pre-academic skills may be necessary for children who are very young or delayed in development. Examples of the types of skills to be assessed include matching ability (beginning with three-dimensional objects, and moving to colors, shapes, and pictures), identifying visual similarities and differences, understanding basic quantitative concepts (e.g., "big," "little"), and matching and identification of letters and numbers. We prefer to use commercially available educational toys for toddlers to assess many of these skills. Color matching is painless when children are asked to sort a pile of different colored socks into pairs. Graduated nesting cups can help determine whether or not the youngster has a sense of early quantitative concepts. Pictures of a variety of different types of trucks, bottles, and balls can be used to determine whether or not the child can categorize these by generic concept rather than visuo-spatial features.*

Motor Ability. In preschool children, identification of motor delays can be an important diagnostic indicator of neurological delay or dysfunction. Formal measures of motor skills (e.g., the Bayley) are available for very young children, and a motor domain on a variety of developmental inventories, such as the Vineland or the Battelle,

---

*The second author is indebted to her colleagues Reiko Simmons and Emelia Sica for these creative assessment techniques with young and multihandicapped children.

provides a good estimate of motor functioning for older preschoolers. Interpretation of an observed delay in motor skills must be made within the context of other findings, especially cognitive tasks that do not require a motor response. In many cases of neurologic impairment in young children, delays are evident across all skill areas; hence, the motor deficit is not of specific concern, but is symptomatic of a general developmental delay. However, in other cases of motor delay due to neurologic causes, cognitive skills may be unaffected. Care must be taken in such instances to avoid an erroneous diagnosis of mental retardation on the basis of noncognitive motor delays (Kearsley, 1981).

Sensory Ability. As with older children, the purpose of the sensory examination in preschool youngsters is to identify any sensory deficits of educational significance. Formal assessment of hearing and vision in preschoolers is best left to specialists, although the clinician certainly should note any behaviors that may suggest the presence of such problems. We continue to be surprised by the degree to which basic sensory deficits are overlooked in very young children and the ways in which the often bizarre behaviors associated with these conditions are explained away or attributed to other, generally psychological, causes. Recently the second author evaluated a 4-year-old youngster who had been identified as mentally retarded on the basis of a Binet IQ score of 36. In the report of that evaluation, the psychologist had commented that the child was "remarkably verbal" given his level of intellectual ability. After spending a few moments with the youngster, it was apparent that the boy was not making use of vision: he did not appear to see the pictures, and even misidentified his mother twice in the waiting room, approaching another woman instead. A completely verbal scale that, unlike the Binet, did not require the use of visual stimuli, revealed an IQ score within the low average range. A subsequent neurologic evaluation confirmed our suspicion of occipital lobe dysfunction resulting in a severe visual impairment. This anecdote illustrates the importance of attending to apparent discrepancies in young children's behavior, such as this young man's "remarkable verbal skill." In this case, his verbal skill reflected his true ability, and his failure to identify pictures and succeed on other tasks on the Binet was due to his visual impairment.

Although older preschoolers may be capable of performing on some of the sensory-perceptual tasks referred to in Chapter 3, for most younger children assessment must rely on more informal measures, such as observation and parent interview. A feeding problem like avoiding textured foods may be evidence of sensory impairment. The same is true of youngsters who dislike tactile stimulation such as cuddling or light tickling, or who protest during such activities as bathing, hair washing or combing, or sand play. In contrast to these hypersensitive youngsters are those who exhibit possible indicators of hyposensitive types of neurologic impairment and require aggressive stimulation for a response.

Social Behavior and Temperament. As noted earlier, neurologic dysfunction is not expressed only in cognitive or motor domains, but may be associated with some atypical behavior patterns as well (Rothbart & Posner, 1985). In preschool children, such behavior patterns are often referred to as qualities of *temperament*, a term used to describe the variations of behavior in such areas as activity level, frustration tolerance, and desire for physical contact (Buss & Plomin, 1975; Schaffer & Emerson, 1964). Longitudinal studies such as those of Thomas and Chess (1977) have reported that about 10% of children possess what they call a "difficult child" temperament, associated with low frustration tolerance, resistance to physical contact, and resistance to a caregiver's attempts to provide comfort.

Assessment of atypical behavior in very young children may rely on temperament checklists like those prepared by Carey and McDevitt (1977). Mary Giffin (1981) has identified behavioral indicators of possible psychopathology in infants and toddlers that can be identified through systematic observation of the child interacting with the parent or primary caregiver. For older preschoolers, formal teacher or parent checklists - such as the California Preschool Social Competency Scale and the Child Behavior Checklist - are viable alternatives.

Self-Care Skills. A major task of the preschool stage is the mastery of daily living skills such as feeding, dressing, and toileting. Failure to master these skills at age-appropriate levels may indicate general developmental delay. However, if self-care skills are uniquely depressed, a different pattern of neurologic strengths and weaknesses, such as a motor or sensory impairment, may be suggested. Many youngsters who have such impairments have difficulty mastering the use of feeding utensils and continue to rely on finger feeding as late as 4 or 5 years of age. Because balance, directionality, and finger and hand strength may be poorly developed in children with neurologic impairment, dressing may be uniquely difficult and toileting, which relies to a large extent on dressing as a prerequisite skill, may be delayed as well. Assessment of self-care skills generally relies on a parent report scale, such as the Vineland Adaptive Behavior Scale, or one of the developmental inventories that includes self-care skills as a separate domain (e.g., Minnesota Child Development Inventory [MCDI], Battelle Developmental Inventory [BDI], Developmental Profile).

Neuropsychologically Relevant Tasks. Few tasks developed for preschool children have been validated specifically for identifying neurologic dysfunction. Although the identification of left-right differences remains one of the more potent indicators of neuropsychological impairment in children (Selz & Reitan, 1981), few of the standardized tasks employed for this purpose with older children are appropriate for youngsters much below age 5. However, several informal strategies have been used by the authors to identify lateral asymmetries. One such procedure utilizes the pegboard task on the Bayley and determines over a number of trials whether there is a consistent hand preference observed and whether or not any systematic neglect of one end of the pegboard or the other occurs. The motor speed of the two hands can be compared by having the child complete the pegboard with the left and right hands separately. Although grip strength using the hand dynamometer is not viable with preschool children, a gross estimate of the relative strength of the two hands can be made by asking the child to squeeze the examiner's index fingers with the preferred and nonpreferred hands. Asymmetry of young children's figure drawings may reveal some systematic hemispace neglect of lateralizing significance (Telzrow & L. C. Hartlage, 1983).

Also relevant is evidence that unilateral lesions occurring at a very young age may not manifest the same lateralizing findings expressed in older children or adults (K. B. Fitzhugh et al., 1962). Thus, although some basic motor or sensory asymmetries may be identified on some of the tasks described above, the degree to which these are reflected in associated asymmetries of higher cortical skills (e.g., language versus visuo-spatial abilities) is questionable. Our best advice in such situations is to report the observed asymmetries and comment on their possible implications. We then provide interventions designed to develop skills associated with the impaired brain regions, because the suggestion of limited progress that would be true of an older child may not apply to the preschool population.

One task developed largely as a research tool has been used clinically by the second author in identifying neurologically based deficits in preschool children (Telzrow, 1983). A reaction time device developed by Jensen (1980) has correlated at significant levels with IQ and academic achievement in adults (Jensen, 1980; Vernon, 1981, 1985) and has been associated with hard measures of neurologic integrity, such as evoked potentials (Jensen, Schafer, & Crinella, 1981). Intelligence, therefore, partially reflects the speed of information processing based on biological neuronal connections. Performance is unaffected by practice or experience, and may accurately measure the biological integrity of the central nervous system. The task in question has been taught successfully to children as young as 2-1/2 years, and significant negative correlations with Peabody Picture Vocabulary Test (PPVT) scores have been reported for preschoolers (Telzrow, 1983). This type of task may help ascertain whether observed deficits are associated with inexperience or a specific response format inherent in the task, or whether such children may have comprehensive dysfunction of the central nervous system.

SUMMARY

Neuropsychological assessment of preschool children follows the same general format outlined for older youngsters, although greater reliance must be placed on observation and parent-report data, given the limited number of directly measurable abilities in the preschool population. Formal, validated measures of brain-behavior relationships have not been developed for very young children. As a result, examiners must employ an interpretive model that incorporates knowledge of preschool development and neuropsychological functioning. The case studies that follow illustrate how diagnostic inferences might be derived from available test data. Recommendations for intervention are included with each case illustration.

CASE STUDY #1

HYPERLEXIA WITH RECEPTIVE AND EXPRESSIVE LANGUAGE DISORDERS.
(Thomas, black male, age 5-1)

Background and Observation:

Thomas is a tall, sturdy 5-year-old who has been identified as having delayed language. He has attended a special needs preschool and was referred for evaluation to assist in further educational planning for him.

Mrs. F reported Thomas was the product of a normal pregnancy. Labor was long and inconsistent, but otherwise delivery was normal. Mrs. F described Thomas as an active, alert infant whose physical developmental milestones occurred on schedule. She indicated Thomas began to use single words before he was 1 year old, but these were unclear, and he did not combine words into phrases until approximately age 3. Thomas's health history has been unremarkable, and he takes no medication.

Mr. and Mrs. F have three other children, all younger than Thomas. Both parents have college degrees. Mrs. F did not know of any history of learning problems in the family, although she said her husband may have been somewhat slow to talk. Both parents are right-handed, as is Thomas.

Thomas's teacher described him as a pleasant, cooperative child who wants to please. She indicated his self-care skills are relatively well-developed, but he demonstrates difficulty in both understanding and using language. Much of Thomas's spontaneous speech appears to be structured, automatic phrases he has acquired from others. He receives speech therapy twice per week with one other child.

In a classroom observation Thomas appeared alert and attentive to a calendar activity. He correctly identified the number 17 on the calendar. In a questioning game Thomas demonstrated some difficulty using question forms, particularly with the correct use of pronouns and

articles (e.g., he stated "Is you food?" and "Is it animal?").
Thomas participated in a movement game, appearing alert
and involved. During free play he gravitated to the play
area, where he was observed to engage in an elaborate
make-believe role, dressing in an apron and preparing a
meal, gesturing to dolls as he made his way around the
kitchen.

Thomas accompanied the examiner willingly and was
attentive and cooperative throughout two testing sessions.
Initially he appeared to be shy or embarrassed, turning
his body and face away from the examiner and covering
his face or averting his gaze. However, this behavior
ended after a few moments of interaction. Thomas's
speech was characterized by word finding problems
interspersed with bursts of choppy, explosive word
combinations. His speech had a telegraphic nature, with
many articles and verb forms omitted. A tendency to add
the plural "s" to words when the singular would be correct
was observed (e.g., he called a picture of a chair "chairs"
and a picture of a boy "boys"). When Thomas could not
find the correct word, he either gave a clearly incorrect,
unrelated answer, as if he must say something, *anything*,
or he gave an association to the stimulus. An example of
the first type of response was his naming several objects
"boys" or "dogs" in a perseverative fashion. Examples of
the other type of response are saying "dangerous" and
then "fire engine" to a picture of a ladder, and "cup" to a
picture of a thermos. Despite his early shyness, Thomas
subsequently became more expressive, and interacted a
great deal nonverbally. He made eye contact and showed
great enthusiasm and pleasure upon successful completion
of various tasks.

Test Results:

Kaufman Assessment Battery for Children (K-ABC)

Sequential	SS	Simultaneous	SS
Hand Movements	7	Gestalt Closure	7
Number Recall	8	Triangles	8
Word Order	7	Matrix Analogies	9
		Spatial Memory	5
Sequential = 83±7		Simultaneous = 81±7	

Mental Processing Composite = 80±6

Nonverbal Score = 81±7

These results suggest that Thomas's general intellectual level is below average, equivalent to the 9th percentile of the population. There is no significant difference between sequential and simultaneous processing abilities shown by his performance on the K-ABC, nor are there any significant strengths or weaknesses demonstrated on the subtest analysis. Because the K-ABC does not have heavy language demands, and because the K-ABC nonverbal score is nearly identical to Thomas's MPC, it does not seem likely that a specific language disorder resulted in artifactually depressed scores. However, a nonverbal scale of cognitive ability was administered to provide further information about Thomas's processing skills.

Leiter International Performance Scale

Thomas achieved a basal age on the Leiter at year 4, passed three subtests at year 5, one subtest at year 6, and obtained a ceiling at year 7. His resulting mental age on the Leiter was 5-3, with a derived IQ score of 102. These results, within the average range of intellectual ability, are significantly higher than Thomas's performance on the K-ABC. It appears that the types of tasks on the Leiter, especially at the early levels, are ones on which Thomas excels (e.g., visual matching). As items required more reasoning and concept formation, he experienced difficulty. Because the K-ABC Nonverbal Scale comprises different sorts of tasks (e.g., memory of sequences of hand movements, nonverbal analogies, and visuo-spatial construction and memory), this may explain the difference in scores between the two measures.

K-ABC Achievement Scale

Subtest	SS	Age Equivalent
Expressive Vocabulary	68±9	2-9
Faces & Places	(W)74±11	2-6
Arithmetic	107±8	5-6
Riddles	(W)76±10	3-0
Reading/Decoding	(S)144±6	7-3
Reading/Understanding	--	7-6

It is apparent from examining these scores that Thomas exhibits a unique pattern of strengths and weaknesses. Although his ability to name objects (Expressive Vocabulary), to identify objects from a verbal description (Riddles), and to identify common nursery rhyme and television characters (Faces & Places) are all significantly below his chronological age, his performance on arithmetic tasks is at age level, and he demonstrates superior ability to decode words. This variability in scores can be attributed to differences in auditory-verbal use of language, with which Thomas had extreme difficulty, and written orthographic features of language, for which he shows a unique and precocious ability. Thomas's word recognition score, at the 99.8 percentile, is in the superior range. Though no standard score could be derived for his chronological age on the Reading/Understanding subtest because it is not designed for children under age 7, it is apparent from the age score of 7-6 that Thomas understands at least some of what he reads. An analysis of Thomas's performance on the Arithmetic subtest suggests that his identification of number symbols, counting, and other skills typically associated with mathematics computation tends to be superior to the development of mathematical concepts, such as quantity.

Boder Test of Reading/Spelling Patterns

Thomas's reading quotient on the Boder (word recognition only) was 135, consistent with his performance on the K-ABC. He spelled 80% of the known words correctly , but spelled only 20% of unknown words as good phonic equivalents (GFEs). This pattern of spelling errors provides further evidence that Thomas has a unique facility for retaining and recalling the orthographic features of words he has seen, though his sound-symbol abilities are not developed. He could not correctly identify any letter sounds, and his attempts to spell unknown words were characterized by random sequences of letters (e.g., hundred/conoex, does/meed, city/ooov). The unknown words Thomas did spell as GFEs were words he had encountered before, and he spelled them perfectly, as he did with the known words. To further illustrate the precocity of Thomas's ability to learn the surface structure of words, the examiner wrote her name and the name of a visiting colleague on a piece of paper; Thomas looked at the names for less than 1 minute and was able to write them correctly without looking as long as 1 hour later.

Developmental Profile

Domain	Age Equivalent
Physical	3-4
Self-Help	5-2
Social	3-8
Academic	4-8
Communication	2-4

These scores demonstrate once again the patterns of strengths and weaknesses in Thomas's functioning. Although self-help skills are commensurate with Thomas's chronological age, mild to severe delays are noted in most other areas, most notably communication.

Minnesota Child Development Inventory (MCDI)

Domain	Age Equivalent
General Development	4-6
Gross Motor	2-9
Fine Motor	4-3
Expressive Language	2-6
Comprehension-Conceptual	4-6
Situation Comprehension	4-0
Self-Help	5-9
Personal-Social	3-0

These results, which are consistent with the findings on the Developmental Profile, reflect the variability in Thomas's skill areas. Weakest domains appear to be gross motor and expressive language, while self-care skills represent a strength. General development is approximately 8 months below Thomas's chronological age, although the wide range in his abilities makes an average score misleading.

Developmental Test of Visual Motor Integration (VMI)

Thomas completed six forms, for an age score of 4-4 and a standard score of 8 ($M = 10$, $SD = 3$).

Child Behavior Checklist (CBCL)-Parent Edition

Mrs. F responded to the CBCL items comparing Thomas's behavior to that of other children. Her responses indicated Thomas's behavior is within normal limits when compared with other children his age and sex.

Finger Oscillation

While the level of Thomas's performance on the electric tapper was within normal limits (RH = 40 taps/10 seconds; LH = 32 taps/10 seconds), the pattern of performance showed depressed left-hand tapping relative to right.

Summary and Recommendations:

Thomas is a cooperative, pleasant young man who is large for his age. He demonstrated good ability to concentrate and focus both during the testing situation and during a classroom observation. Although his spontaneous, meaningful language is severely limited, Thomas can communicate well nonverbally and is expressive and socially appropriate in this regard.

Thomas is specifically weak in understanding and using spoken language. This deficiency is exaggerated by overstimulation, at which point he appears confused, upset, and his responses become random. It seems likely this language disorder is associated with chronic neuropsychological dysfunction.

In contrast to the spoken language deficits, Thomas demonstrates a precocious ability to retain, use, and recall written language. He is able to decode words at least 2 years above his chronological age and seems to comprehend words at this level. Thomas can visually imprint and produce words he has seen only briefly, regardless of type face. Even though he comprehends what he reads now, it is uncertain whether his comprehension will keep pace with his decoding skills as he gets older.

Developmental testing suggests Thomas's self-care abilities are age appropriate, although physical and social development are mildly delayed, with language showing significant delays. Cognitive assessment is inconsistent, but it is suggested that for now school officials presume Thomas has average intellectual ability with specific language impairment. It will become easier to make a determination about the level of Thomas's intellectual ability as he grows older.

These results suggest Thomas may benefit from an educational program that is as follows:

1. Responsive to the variability in his developmental areas - mainly, fostering growth in language and social development while responding to his age appropriate self-care skills.
2. Able to incorporate supplemental techniques to reinforce his understanding and use of language. Examples include written language, total communication, pictures, and manipulatives.
3. Able to foster the development of daily living skills involving speech (e.g., understanding and using question forms; identifying name, address, sex, age, etc.; relating experiences spontaneously).
4. Able to encourage the development of deep structure (i.e., meaning, comprehension) in reading, while weaning Thomas from his pre-occupation with surface structure features.

Thomas demonstrates a complex neuropsychological pattern of strengths and weaknesses, and ongoing monitoring of his progress is recommended. A formal evaluation is advised prior to school age and before any program change is made.

CASE STUDY #2

RECEPTIVE AND EXPRESSIVE LANGUAGE DELAY. (Janet, white female, age 5-11)

Background and Observation:

Janet is a 5-year-old whose kindergarten teacher expressed concern about her ability to understand and use language. An interview with Janet's mother indicated that Mrs. K had significant problems in school, and completed formal education through the seventh grade in special classes. It was apparent in talking with Mrs. K that she exhibits some language problems such as dysnomia and marked circumlocution. Mrs. K lives alone with Janet and Janet's 3-year-old sister. Mrs. K reported she does not read, and that her mother lives close enough to her to help her with her bills and other written information. According to available records, Janet had no formal educational experiences prior to entering kindergarten.

Testing was conducted on two different days; the first session was held in the building where Janet attends kindergarten, and the second day of testing was conducted in the clinic setting. Janet's affect was highly variable during evaluation. At times she was attentive and responsive, but at other times, for no apparent reason, she withdrew, was unresponsive, and appeared to refuse tasks. Previous evaluators have reported similar behavior, and Mrs. K also confirmed that Janet on occasion demonstrates such reactions.

Test Results:

Kaufman Assessment Battery for Children (K-ABC)

Sequential	SS	Simultaneous	SS
Hand Movements	2	Gestalt Closure	8
Number Recall	5	Triangles	8
Word Order	8	Matrix Analogies	8
		Spatial Memory	12

Sequential = 71±7   Simultaneous = 93±7

Mental Processing Composite = 80±6

Nonverbal Score = 83±6

These results demonstrate significant variability in Janet's mental processing abilities. Although the Hand Movements subtest represents a significant weakness for Janet, Spatial Memory is a particular strength. In general, Janet performed better on Simultaneous than Sequential tasks: the 22-point difference between the Simultaneous and Sequential Processing scores is significant at the $p<.01$ level. This pattern of scores suggests that Janet may have unique difficulty processing information in a sequential, step-by-step fashion. Because language is a sequential process, this cognitive deficit may be associated with Janet's language disorder.

Stanford-Binet Intelligence Scale

The Binet was administered to verify results obtained on the K-ABC and as another measure of intellectual ability. Janet obtained a basal age at year 3-0, and ceiling at year 4-6. This resulted in a mental age of 3-5 that, when considered with Janet's chronological age of 5-11, yields an IQ score of 48. There is clinical evidence that this score seriously underestimates Janet's actual intellectual ability. Janet's poor performance on the Binet can be attributed to the following: (a) poor development of language and language concepts, which are necessary for success on such tasks as Comparison of Balls, Response to Pictures, Comprehension, Opposite Analogies, and so on; and (b) evidence of passive-aggressive behavior, resulting in refusal of some tasks that did appear to be within Janet's ability to respond.

K-ABC Achievement Battery

Subtest	SS
Faces & Places	69±11
Arithmetic	89±8
Riddles	64±10
Reading/Decoding	97±6

These results reflect Janet's specific cognitive strengths and weaknesses, as well as the experiences she has had. The two lowest subtests, Faces & Places and Riddles, both constitute significantly weak areas when compared with her overall achievement levels. Riddles, a subtest on which Janet received a raw score of 0, requires listening ability and language processing and integration. Faces & Places is a general information task that may have been depressed by Janet's inexperience with stimuli of this sort.

Janet scored significantly higher on the Arithmetic and Reading/Decoding subtests. These relatively good scores probably reflect the good teaching Janet has had in kindergarten. In addition, because early letter and number identification rely on simultaneous processing abilities, a relative strength for Janet, her elevated scores on these subtests may be attributed to her greater ability to benefit from instruction on tasks emphasizing visuo-spatial, holistic processing. Janet's pattern of errors on the K-ABC tasks demonstrates her strength in visuo-spatial processing, and, conversely, her weakness in sequential, linguistic processing. She correctly identified numerals through 17, but had some difficulty with such concepts as "more than," "less than," and so on. She correctly identified most letters out of context. Janet wrote the alphabet correctly in order, wrote numerals 1-10 dictated by the examiner, and wrote her name.

Developmental Test of Visual Motor Integration (VMI)

Janet correctly formed the first nine designs, which resulted in an age score of 5-4 and a standard score of 8 ($M = 10$, $SD = 3$). These results suggest that Janet's difficulties are rather specific to language-related and sequential, linguistic processing abilities rather than a general developmental delay.

Devereux Elementary School Behavior Rating Scale II

Janet's teacher responded to the Devereux items. Three of the 16 areas were rated significantly different from average children Janet's age. According to her teacher, Janet needs more than an average amount of direction in doing work, is slower to get started and less self-directed than her peers, and demonstrates more perseverance than average.

Vineland Social Maturity Scale

Mrs. K responded to the Vineland items about Janet's ability to care for herself and interact with others and the environment. Mrs. K's responses resulted in an age score of 4.7 and a social quotient of 79. Janet's mother reported she does not relate experiences, tends not to perform for others, and is not allowed outside the yard because of her inability to communicate. She can bathe herself, can care for her own toileting needs, and goes to bed alone.

Finger Oscillation

Though right-handed, Janet's performance showed no difference between the two hands (RH = 27 taps/10 seconds; LH = 27 taps/10 seconds). Janet's depressed right-hand finger tapping is consistent with the pattern of psychometric test results suggesting pervasive language deficiency, as in chronic left hemisphere dysfunction.

Summary and Recommendations:

Janet is an attractive, dark-haired, sturdy-looking 5-year-old whose history suggests marked language delay. Current test results suggest that Janet has unique difficulty processing information in a sequential manner. Intellectual testing suggests language production and comprehension of concepts are significantly delayed. Neuropsychological screening and the pattern of mental processing abilities are consistent with a specific neuropsychological disorder affecting language and related mental processes.

Janet shows relative strengths in processing information in a holistic, gestalt manner, such as in pictures, symbols, and pictographs. This skill is reflected in her age-appropriate identification of letters and numbers.

Janet's adaptive behavior, according to her mother's responses, is a bit more than 1 year behind her chronological age. It seems likely that Janet's language deficits have resulted in some difficulty in acquiring age-appropriate skills in a number of areas. There also is a possibility Mrs. K may be somewhat oversolicitous with Janet, which also may have resulted in some delays in acquiring independent behaviors.

These results suggest that Janet could benefit from a developmentally appropriate program that can respond to her unique deficits in language-related areas without delaying her progress in stronger skills. Instructional strategies emphasizing visuo-spatial features of stimuli may be used as a basis for introducing language concepts and teaching vocabulary and syntax. Janet also could benefit from a highly experiential approach to learning basic skills. As she matures and educational demands call for increased emphasis on sequential, linguistic skills, continued appraisal of Janet's progress is recommended in the event more compensatory approaches become appropriate.

REFERENCES

Buss, A. H., & Plomin, R. (1975). *A Temperament Theory of Personality Development*. New York: John Wiley & Sons.

Carey, W. B., & McDevitt, S. C. (1977). *Infant Temperament Questionnaire.* Unpublished manuscript. (Available from W. B. Carey, 319 W. Front Street, Media, PA 19063)

Coplan, J. (1982). Parental estimate of child's developmental level in a high-risk population. *American Journal of Diseases in Children, 136,* 101-104.

Dale, P. S. (1976). *Language Development: Structure and Function* (2nd ed.). New York: Holt, Rinehart, & Winston.

Dreisbach, M., & Keogh, B. K. (1982). Test-wiseness as a factor in readiness test performance of young Mexican-American children. *Journal of Educational Psychology, 74,* 224-229.

Drotar, D., Baskiewicz, N., Irving, N., Kennell, J., & Klaus, M. (1975). The adaptation of parents to the birth of an infant with a congenital malformation: A hypothetical model. *Pediatrics, 56,* 710-717.

Evans, R., & Sparrow, M. (1976). Some new departures in the assessment of early childhood development. *Association of Educational Psychologists Journal, 4,* 14-20.

Fitzhugh, K. B., Fitzhugh, L. C., & Reitan, R. M. (1962). Wechsler-Bellevue comparison in groups with "chronic" and "current" lateralized and diffuse brain lesions. *Journal of Consulting Psychology, 26,* 306-310.

Giffin, M. (1981). Assessing infant and toddler development. In B. Weissbourd & J. Musick (Eds.), *Infants: Their Social Environments* (pp. 48-63). Washington, DC: National Association for the Education of Young Children.

Hartlage, L. C., Stovall, K. W., & Hartlage, P. L. (1980). Age related neuropsychological sequelae of Reye's Syndrome. *Clinical Neuropsychology, 2,* 83-86.

Horton, K. B. (1974). Infant intervention and language learning. In R. L. Schiefelbusch & L. L. Lloyd (Eds.), *Language Perspectives: Acquisition, Retardation, and Intervention* (pp. 469-491). Baltimore: University Park Press.

Jensen, A. R. (1980). Chronometric analysis of intelligence. *Journal of Social and Biological Structures, 3,* 103-122.

Jensen, A. R., Schafer, E. W., & Crinella, F. M. (1981). Reaction time, evoked brain potentials, and psychometric g in the severely retarded. *Intelligence, 5,* 179-197.

Kearsley, K. B. (1981). Cognitive assessment of the handicapped infant: The need for an alternative approach. *American Journal of Orthopsychiatry, 51*, 43-54.

Klonoff, H., Low, M. D., & Clark, C. (1977). Head injuries in children: A prospective five year follow-up. *Journal of Neurology, Neurosurgery, and Psychiatry, 40*, 1211-1219.

Lazar, I., & Darlington, R. B. (1978). *Lasting Effects after Preschool* (DHEW Publication No. OHDS 79-30178). Washington, DC: Office of Human Development Services.

Moses, K. (1984). *Impairment in Children: Growth through Grieving*. Evanston, IL: Resource Network, Inc.

Reuter, J., Stancin, T., & Craig, P. (1981). *Kent Scoring Adaptation of the Bayley Scales of Infant Development*. Kent, OH: Kent Developmental Metrics, Inc.

Rosenberg, J. B., & Weller, G. M. (1973). Minor physical anomalies and academic performance in young school-children. *Developmental Medicine and Child Neurology, 15*, 131-135.

Rothbart, M. K., & Posner, M. I. (1985). Temperament and the development of self-regulation. In L. C. Hartlage & C. F. Telzrow (Eds.), *The Neuropsychology of Individual Differences: A Developmental Perspective* (pp. 93-123). New York: Plenum.

Sattler, J. M. (1982). *Assessment of Children's Intelligence and Special Abilities*. Boston: Allyn & Bacon.

Schaffer, H. R., & Emerson, P. E. (1964). Patterns of response to physical contact in early human development. *Journal of Child Psychology and Psychiatry, 5*, 1-13.

Schweinhart, L. J., & Weikart, D. P. (1980). *Young Children Grow Up: The Effects of the Perry Preschool Program on Youths through Age 15*. Ypsilanti, MI: Monographs of the High/Scope Education Research Foundation.

Selz, M., & Reitan, R. M. (1981). Rules for neuropsychological diagnosis: Classification of brain function in older children. *Journal of Consulting and Clinical Psychology, 47*, 258-264.

Telzrow, C. F. (1983). Making child neuropsychological appraisal appropriate for children: Alternatives to downward extension of adult batteries. *Clinical Neuropsychology, 5*, 136-141.

Telzrow, C. F., & Hartlage, L. C. (1983). Evaluation and programming for infants and preschoolers with neurological and neuropsychological impairments. In C. R. Reynolds & J. H. Clark (Eds.), *Assessment and Programming for Children with Low-Incidence Handicaps* (pp. 43-118). New York: Plenum.

Thomas, A., & Chess, S. (1977). *Temperament and Development.* New York: Brunner/Mazel, Inc.

Vernon, P. A. (1981). Reaction time and intelligence in the mentally retarded. *Intelligence, 5,* 345-355.

Vernon, P. A. (1985). Individual differences in general cognitive ability. In L. C. Hartlage & C. F. Telzrow (Eds.), *The Neuropsychology of Individual Differences: A Development Perspective* (pp. 125-150). New York: Plenum.

Waldrop, M. F., & Halverson, C. F. (1971). Minor physical anomalies and hyperactive behavior in young children. In J. Hellmuth (Ed.), *The Exceptional Infant* (Vol. 2, pp. 343-380). New York: Brunner/Mazel.

Waldrop, M. F., Pederson, F. A., & Bell, R. Q. (1968). Minor physical anomalies and behavior in preschool children. *Child Development, 39,* 391-400.

5

ASSESSMENT OF NEURODEVELOPMENTAL PROBLEMS IN SCHOOL-AGED CHILDREN

INTRODUCTION

There are a number of childhood neurodevelopmental problems that are appropriate for neuropsychological assessment because of their comparatively high incidence or their potential for developmental handicap. Learning problems have long been a special area of interest and application in child clinical neuropsychology. However, neuropsychological contributions to other neurodevelopmental problem areas are increasingly being recognized. In addition to the greater attention given to the neuropsychological aspects of many medical conditions, more psychologists are now in settings where their interactions with physicians, school personnel, and families enable them to contribute to the assessment and general management planning to help minimize or alleviate some of the problems associated with these conditions.

HEAD INJURY

Although head trauma is a major cause of morbidity and mortality, there have not been good incidence estimates of its frequency (Annegers, Grabow, Kurland, & Louis, 1980). Relatively recent data suggest almost 10 million such injuries in a given year, with the vast majority considered mild. These injuries are proportionately more frequent among children than adults, with boys at a 3:1 risk ratio relative to the general population (Boll, 1982; Caveness, 1977; Craft, 1972; Goethe & Levin, 1984; McLean, Temkin, Dikmen, & Wyler, 1983).

Although the general belief has been that children's brains will recover more fully from injury due to their greater plasticity (Alajouanine & Lhermitte, 1965; Black, Jeffries, Blumer, Wellner, & Walker, 1969; Bruce, Schut, Bruno, Woods, & Sutton, 1978; E. H. Lenneberg & E. Lenneberg, 1975), recent research has suggested that young children may be more affected with respect to memory and cognition (Levin, Eisenberg, Wigg, & Kobayashi, 1982) and a wide range of adaptive abilities (Cermack, 1985). Another traditional belief is that unilateral damage to a child's brain may not result in the same sorts of language versus spatial deficits that may occur after unilateral cerebral damage in adults (Hecaen, 1976; E. Lenneberg, 1967; Marie, 1922/1971). Again, more recent work does not support this view (Aram, Ekelman, Rose, & Whitaker, 1985; Rankin, Aram, & Horowitz, 1981), suggesting instead that significant damage to the speech area in a child's brain, for example, may result in similar language problems as in adults (Power & Hartlage, 1984).

Memory appears to be the cognitive function most consistently affected by head injury (Benton, 1979; Brooks, 1972, 1974; Hannay, Levin, & Grossman, 1979; Smith, 1974; Squire & Slater, 1975; Thomsen, 1977). However, there is considerable evidence that generalized intellectual impairment follows severe craniocerebral trauma in childhood (Winogren, Knights, & Bawden, 1983), with substantial cognitive impairment most likely to occur after bilateral damage (Rutter, 1981) and more specific loss associated with unilateral damage, depending on locus of the damage (Aram et al., 1985; Yeni-Komshian, 1977). Because memory impairment often follows head injury in children, it is important to include a sufficient number of test items sensitive to this phenomenon. Further, because most cognitive functions require some degree of memory, it is also important to keep in mind the possible role of memory dysfunction in the child's performance on given psychometric measures dependent on memory.

A more subtle but equally important effect of closed head injury involves personality and behavior change (Power & Hartlage, 1982). Such phenomena as poor concentration, fatigue, and irritability have been long recognized as common features of post-concussive syndrome (Jennett, 1978; Rutherford, Merrett, & McDonald, 1977), and in recent years there has been evidence of a diverse range of other behavioral sequelae such as euphoria, social withdrawal, hostility, anxiety, silliness, social crudeness, lability of affect, disinhibition, reduced initiative, and blunting of emotion (Boll, 1982). Not surprisingly, following even mild head injury there is a marked increase in the likelihood of special class placement, even among children who had been academically and socially adjusted prior to the head injury (Klonoff, Low, & Clark, 1977). A recent fairly comprehensive study of behavioral sequelae of mild head injury found more than 90% incidence of tiredness, short temper, depression, and being easily upset, and more than 80% incidence of agitation, anger, confusion, discouragement, forgetfulness, and being less happy (Hartlage, 1985). When parental reports of children's behavior changes following head injury were compared with self-reports, the incidence of change was even higher. Parents reported change on more than 50 items, suggesting they recognize the extent of behavioral differences to a greater degree than the children (Hartlage, 1985).

Finally, a corollary sequel to much head injury in children during a period of a few months to 2 years involves temporary difficulty with the levels of concentration and mental stamina required for satisfactory school performance. There is a danger that a child whose school performance is poor following a head injury may be labeled as "lazy" or "spoiled by all the attention he got after the injury," and punished for academic performance at levels lower than those comparable to pre-injury levels. Sustained mental effort at a level necessary for satisfactory school performance may be impaired for many months following even a mild head injury, and the psychologist can provide a most important service to the child by informing parents and teachers of this phenomenon.

EPILEPSY

Epilepsy is primarily a childhood disorder with approximately 90% of all epileptic patients developing their initial symptoms before the teenage years are completed. Prevalence rates have been estimated as ranging from 4.4 to 5.8 per thousand in the age range 0-9, and from 3.4 to 6.6 in the older childhood ages (Epilepsy Foundation of America, 1975). There are two risk periods when epilepsy is most likely to appear - during the first few years of life and at the onset of puberty. When epilepsy occurs early in life it may be related to cerebral damage that occurred either prenatally or at birth, whereas the etiology of onset at later ages is often less clear (Livingstone, 1972). Thus the neuropsychological findings in children may range from clear evidence of fairly global cerebral dysfunction to essentially normal findings, so that there is no characteristic profile among children who suffer seizures. In some cases children may develop seizures secondary to a specific brain lesion, and there may be more focal or localizing signs of brain impairment. However, such findings are more related to the underlying brain damage than to the actual symptom (i.e., epilepsy) of this damage.

Historically, seizures have been classified into three major types, generally referred to as *grand mal*, *petit mal*, and *psychomotor* seizures. Recently there has been a trend toward reclassification, using terms of *generalized tonic-clonic*, *absence*, and *partial complex* to describe seizure types that correspond, somewhat respectively, to the historic classification. In the generalized tonic-clonic seizure, there may be loss of consciousness, sometimes precipitated by a prodromal warning or aura, with alternating rigidity and rapid jerking of the muscles. Frequently the child may be disoriented, lethargic, or tired following the seizure. In the partial complex seizure, which may appear more frequently in the older child, there may be abnormal behavior such as chewing movements, lip smacking, or some stereotyped behavior such as picking at clothing, without full loss of consciousness or tonic-clonic movements. With absence attacks, which frequently begin in the preschool to early school ages, and often disappear at puberty, there is apt to be a fairly brief period of altered consciousness during which the child appears to be staring vacantly into space. With such seizures there is usually no prolonged after effect, and the child may resume the pre-seizure activity without recognition of the episode. Although the EEG is the diagnostic procedure most commonly used in the diagnosis of epilepsy, in many cases it appears normal when the child is not experiencing a seizure.

From the child's perspective, the generalized tonic-clonic type of seizure presents many social problems involving the possibility of peer rejection or even ridicule from the dramatic impact of the seizure, as well as from the potential soiling that can occur. Further, many social activities may be precluded by fear of having a seizure while driving, swimming, or other activities common to the age group. The partial complex seizures, though less dramatic, also can cause social problems because the child is seen as strange. The absence variety, though undramatic, can occur with considerable frequency and may lead to special problems in school performance due to the interruptions of consciousness. Studies of children with all types of epilepsy generally have revealed patterns of academic problems that do not appear to relate directly to lowered cognitive functioning (Hartlage & Green, 1971). Parents tend to be overprotective of the child with epilepsy (Hartlage & Green, 1972), and this can cause problems as the child reaches adolescence and may need and demand greater independence.

Although not widely recognized, the use of anticonvulsant medication for seizure treatment and control can cause a number of problems with attention and psychomotor function. Even within therapeutic serum levels, common anticonvulsant medications such as the barbiturates and related drugs can impair these functions, and lower performance on such test items as Wechsler subtests Digit Span and Coding (Hartlage, 1981). Further, such medication occasionally can result in false positive lateralizing signs by comparative lowering of motor performance on tests like rate of rapid finger oscillation on the nondominant hand (Hartlage, 1984). For these reasons it is important when assessing a child with epilepsy to determine the medications with which he or she may be treated, and take into account the possible effects of such medication on test scores.

HYDROCEPHALUS

Hydrocephalus, a condition characterized by an increased volume of cerebrospinal fluid (CSF), may produce enlargement of the head when it develops prior to fusion of the cranial sutures. In cases where hydrocephalus occurs very early, it may be due to a congenital malformation, although occurrence at any age can result from neoplasms and post-traumatic or post-inflammatory lesions. In many cases of congenital hydrocephalus, the infant dies *in utero*, although in most cases the condition does not become apparent for some 2 or 3 months. Once identified, it may be treated surgically by such procedures as shunting. Results from such treatment indicate control in approximately 65% of cases, a fatality rate of 10%, and "normal" children in the range of 25% to 30% (Matthews & Ransohoff, 1968). Other cases do not require surgery and spontaneously arrest without special treatment. Hydrocephalus sometimes is associated with meningomyelocele, which may require combined treatment by such specialties as neurosurgery, orthopedics, pediatrics, psychology, rehabilitation, and urology. With such children, gait may be impaired to the point that a wheelchair is needed (Schulman, 1968).

From a neuropsychological perspective it is important to keep in mind three features of hydrocephalus. First, nearly half of all children with infantile hydrocephalus have associated malformations of the brain (Gilroy & Meyer, 1975). Therefore an evaluation of the child needs to consider this possibility. There generally is a greatly increased risk of impaired intellectual and motor development, and epileptic seizures are relatively common. Second, the surgical destruction of cortical tissue for purposes of inserting the shunt, normally involving the nondominant hemisphere, may result in unilateral impairments to the development of normal patterns of cognitive ability. Because without surgery the survival rate of children born with hydrocephalus is only about 30% at 10 years, most children will have had such shunting (Lorber, 1967). Third, hydrocephalus that occurs later in childhood is likely caused by an underlying insult to the brain, such as a neoplasm, trauma, or infection, and the locus, extent, and type of such insult probably will influence a child's unique neuropsychological profile.

Among the children with hydrocephalus who are not shunted, approximately a fourth may be severely retarded, with a slightly larger percentage showing mental subnormality, and the remainder grossly within the ranges of normality, typically at the lower end of this range. Follow-up of such children has revealed that approximately a third of the total (unshunted) group may be expected to function in a normal school setting (Laurence & Coates, 1967).

A special characteristic of some children with shunted hydrocephalus involves hyperverbal behavior, often described as "the cocktail party personality syndrome." During the evaluation of these children the examiner often describes the child as being highly verbal and may overestimate the child's mental abilities. This over-estimation also is likely to occur in kindergarten, where good socialization skills combined with apparent verbal fluency present an overly optimistic picture that is not sustained in early school grades. On formal measures of intellectual abilities, the performance of these appealing, effervescent children often is below average, even on tests of verbal ability. In general, these children are excessively verbal, but have limited language content, inadequate conceptualization, and superficial social skills. When allowed free rein the children can be impressive, but when interrupted with specific questions requiring conceptual reorganization, the superficiality of their abilities becomes evident. One possible explanation of this phenomenon is that children who have nondominant hemisphere impairment as a residual of the shunting procedure compensate for this limitation by focusing on their comparatively intact verbal skills.

Indirect support for this possibility is provided by a longitudinal follow-up of children who had been shunted at the Medical College of Georgia, with testing done at varying intervals up to early school years. There was a consistent pattern of verbal over nonverbal superiority ranging from an average of 8 to 16 standard score points (dependent on site of the shunt) on such preschool measures as the PPVT compared with the Beery VMI Tests, and on early school-age Wechsler verbal versus performance measures. Even the higher (verbal) standard score equivalents tended to be one or more standard deviations below average, with the lower (nonverbal) equivalent scores bordering around the third percentile, or near the upper limits of mild mental retardation (Hartlage, 1977).

TOURETTE SYNDROME

Gilles de la Tourette syndrome (TS) is an unusual and dramatic tic disorder that emerges during childhood (Dornbush, 1984). Tics represent one of the most common neuropsychiatric disturbances of childhood: By some estimates more than a fourth of all children may suffer from them at one time or another (Golden, 1979). On occasion, multiple muscular tics are accompanied by verbal tics, and this condition represents the constellation referred to as TS. There are special diagnostic problems associated with TS because the symptoms change over time as the tics shift from one body part to another, and the nature and severity of symptoms vary over time (A. K. Shapiro, E. S. Shapiro, Bruun, & Sweet, 1978). In most cases the disorder, although sometimes waning in severity, does not remit spontaneously. Multiple problems are associated with the disorder, with approximately 50% diagnosed as also having attention deficit disorder, and a larger percentage experiencing academic problems, although there is no evidence of lowered general intellectual functioning. A diagnosis of learning disability is made in 20% of TS patients (A. K. Shapiro & E. S. Shapiro, 1982).

Initial symptoms typically involve a single, simple motor tic, usually with first manifestation at an early age; 30% of TS children develop this symptom before school age and 58% by the age of 7 (A. K. Shapiro et al., 1978). This first manifestation is apt to involve an eye blink (35%), head twitch (29%), vocalization in the form of a sound or word (19%), or facial grimace (12%) (A. K. Shapiro & E. S. Shapiro, 1982). From this early manifestation, considerable variability of symptoms is common, although the tendency is for symptoms to proceed in a cephalocaudal direction, spreading to involve the arms, body, and legs (Jagger, Prusoff, Cohen, Kidd, & Carbonari, 1982). Relatively infrequent as a first symptom, vocalizations or noises may be added to or substituted for one or more motor tics. Most frequent noises involve grunting and barking (75%), squeals, high-pitched sounds, shrieks or yelps (62%), or some variant of coughing, throat clearing, snorting, or hissing (59%). Stuttering or stammering, when present (22%), differ from typical patterns of stuttering in that the normal flow of speech is interrupted by muscular contractions, producing either peculiarly accented or unintelligible words (A. K. Shapiro et al., 1978). There tends to be a progression from grunts, barks, and unintelligible sounds to uncontrollable but articulate words or even phrases. The most frequent (and bizarre) vocalization involves coprolalia (33%), although echolalia (31%) and palilalia (29%) are not uncommon.

Coprolalia, although not necessary for a diagnosis of TS in that it occurs in only about a third of cases, is considered a confirmation of the disorder. Because it develops relatively late in the progression of symptoms, with mean onset around 13 to 14 years of age, coprolalia may not be of much diagnostic value in younger children. It is interesting that historic descriptions of coprolalia had incidence percentages up to 65-70% (Abuzzahab & Anderson, 1973; Field, Corbin, Goldstein, & Klass, 1966). The decline in the percentages of children with this symptom may reflect the increasing recognition of the milder forms of the disorder.

Accurate diagnosis is especially relevant for children with TS for two reasons. The symptoms of Tourette syndrome are a source of considerable stress, tension, and distress for afflicted children, resulting in self-consciousness and shame as well as social and educational handicaps; TS children often have few friends, are teased at school, and are apt to withdraw from social interactions (Dornbush, 1984). In a recent study, D. E. Comings and B. G. Comings (1985) concluded that, because of the concomitant behavior and adjustment problems, TS should be considered a psychiatric as well as a neurologic disorder. This conclusion appears warranted, because when symptoms persist and become so severe they hinder educational progress or social development, there is increasing likelihood of developing emotional problems. Psychological involvement in diagnosis allows early and accurate intervention and management; often the presenting symptoms of the neurological disorder are the type for which children are referred to school or clinical psychologists.

A number of investigators have reported neuropsychological deficits in TS, including impaired performance on the Reitan Battery, the Bender-Gestalt, Wechsler Coding, and Wide Range Achievement Test (WRAT) arithmetic subtest (Incagnoli & Kane, 1981). Right cerebral hemisphere abnormalities have been postulated as etiologic by researchers who compared TS children with controls (Sutherland, Kolb, Schoer, Wishaw, & Davies, 1982).

However, the neuropsychological profile of TS is not clear. Previous research, like the studies above, often involves case reports, and the characteristic profile identified has not been confirmed by subsequent control group research. Further, there may be artifacts due to the unique requirements of psychometric tests that obscure the actual nature of the problem. Reported problems involving dyscalculia, for example (Incagnoli & Kane, 1981), may reflect the depression of achievement scores due to motor slowing; a recent study by Dornbush and

Hartlage (1984) demonstrated that, with time limitations removed from the WRAT arithmetic scale, TS children did not manifest dyscalculia relative to a control group. Further, a sample of 28 TS children matched with a control group revealed no pattern of neuropsychological impairments on a very comprehensive battery of neuropsychological tests (Dornbush, 1984). An interesting positive finding in the Dornbush study involved differences between TS and control children on both Conners's scale ratings and Coopersmith Self-Concept ratings by parents and teachers, with the TS children rated significantly lower than controls on all ratings.

There is evidence that low dosages of haloperidol may control or at least alleviate some of the disturbing symptoms, especially the verbal tics. Abuzzahab and Anderson's (1973) survey of the literature found that 89% of symptoms improved after 6 months with haloperidol, compared with 29% for all other treatment modalities. Similar findings were reported by A. K. Shapiro et al. (1978), who found 82.5% success, 8.3% partial success, and 8.3% failures. Another useful drug is clonidine, with a symptom reduction rate only slightly lower (70%) than that for haloperidol. Clonidine treatment reduces behaviors associated with attention deficit and aggressiveness (Cohen, Shaywitz, Caparulo, Young, & Bowers, 1978).

From a psychological perspective, a number of procedures may be helpful. Although the symptoms of Tourette syndrome can be voluntarily suppressed for a period of time, a rebound effect is likely, and attempts to inhibit movements increase tension. This can be alleviated by encouraging the teacher to allow the TS child to be excused on request, so that movement or verbal tics can be expressed in the lavatory or other nondisruptive settings. Support for the child, especially concerning self-concept, may be provided by supportive counseling, social skills enhancement, or other psychotherapeutic approaches. Finally, pressure on the TS child may be relieved by providing counseling for parents and teachers concerning the nature of the disorder and the unique problems it entails.

GENETIC DISORDERS

A number of genetic disorders impair neuropsychological functioning and are increasingly referred for psychological evaluation. An obvious example is trisomy 21 or Down's syndrome, which normally results in depressed mental ability from the mild to moderate retardation levels, but in mosaic form may cause less mental limitation. With an occurrence of approximately one per 2,000 live births among younger parents and one per 20 live births among parents in their 40s, the disorder has become more prevalent with the societal trend toward postponement of childbearing. A further factor in the increased prevalence of Down's syndrome and related disorders is the advance in sophistication and availability of child health services; in the past many children with Down's succumbed to respiratory infection or other problems at relatively early ages. With the combined higher incidence and prevalence of the disorder and public support for providing appropriate educational and social services, many more such children are being seen by psychologists.

Like Down's syndrome, which results from an extra chromosome, genetic disorders reflecting a chromosome abnormality tend to result in global mentally handicapping conditions rather than a unique neuropsychological profile. Other trisomy conditions, such as trisomy 13-15 (D trisomy, Patau's syndrome) and trisomy 17-18 (E trisomy, Edward's syndrome) typically result in severe mental retardation, along with increased incidence of physical stigmata, as in Down's syndrome. Even where a chromosome is only partly damaged, as in partial deletion of the long arm of chromosome 18 or in one of the short arms of a chromosome in the 4-5 group (cri-du-chat syndrome), mental retardation ranges from moderate to profound.

An exception to the general rule of no specific pattern of neuropsychological profile among chromosome disorders is Turner's syndrome, in which the majority of children have only 45 chromosomes (XO). Although a number of physical characteristics and stigmata are present, mental retardation does not necessarily occur; girls with the XO syndrome tend to have uniquely poor spatial abilities, along with increased incidence of hearing difficulty. With milder chromosomal abnormalities like breaks and rearrangements, such conditions as Bloom's syndrome (congenital telangiectatic erythema and stunted growth) may involve less impairment of both global and specific aspects of mental abilities.

Genetic disorders possibly involving gene loci on the X chromosome, such as hyperuricemia with mental retardation (Lesch-Nyhan syndrome), mucopolysaccharidosis II (Hunter's syndrome), and oculocerebrorenal syndrome (Lowe's syndrome) are usually associated with severe global mental retardation, although with Hunter's syndrome the symptoms of mental retardation may be milder and appear later. The behavior of children with Hunter's syndrome is occasionally described as destructive, stubborn, and difficult to control, as opposed to the usual friendly, docile, and happy behavior of trisomy 21 children.

From a diagnostic perspective, psychological assessment is generally requested to obtain a measure of the child's level of mental functioning rather than a diagnosis, although the obtained IQ score may confirm (or reject) a tentative diagnosis. In most cases these sorts of genetic disorders have no specific treatment. Intervention by a medical geneticist or pediatric specialist may be limited to discussing prognosis or recurrence risks in subsequent pregnancies with parents. Psychological intervention would involve developing programming for the child, working with behavior management approaches, or working with families on integrating the handicapped child into family dynamics. To aid in ongoing management and programming, Down's syndrome children may need repeated evaluations over time; there is a general trend toward apparent mental decline from around puberty that may be related to the high incidence of early onset Alzheimer's disease among these children.

DEGENERATIVE DISORDERS

Childhood diseases with progressive impairment, involving either mental or physical decline, represent another category of disorders in which neuropsychological assessment may be requested. More than 600 such diseases have been identified, and there are a variety of ways in which they are classified. Some childhood neurodegenerative diseases may be categorized by their age of onset: infantile (e.g., Tay-Sach's disease), late infantile (e.g., Bielschowsky-Jansky disease), and juvenile (e.g., Speilmeyer-Vogt or Batten's disease). Although such categorization may be helpful for the identification of risk periods for given diseases, the variety of etiologies and clinical features among degenerative diseases with onset at given ages makes it difficult to characterize their course or neuropsychological profile.

Another approach to classification, based mainly on anatomical grounds, groups childrens' degenerative diseases according to whether major clinical or anatomic effects involve the cerebral cortex (polioencephalopathies), subcortical white matter (leukoencephalopathies), or other (e.g., spinocerebellopathies) areas (Dyken & Krawiecki, 1983). This approach to classification includes such disorders as autism and post-vaccine encephalopathy in a single grouping (polioencephalopathies), making it difficult to describe disorders within a given classification in respect to neuropsychological characteristics. Even for classifications based on a specific feature such as breakdown of normal myelin (which includes multiple sclerosis as the most common clinical entity), the neuropsychological profile may be variable. In multiple sclerosis, for example, with onset usually after 10 years of age, there is a tendency for remission and relapse, with decline in visual, frontal lobe, brainstem, and cerebellar functions which can present unique symptoms of neuropsychological impairment at given stages of the disease. Because of these factors, and the tendency for remission and relapse (Gilroy & Meyer, 1975), there is no specific neuropsychologic feature or profile which can be considered specifically diagnostic or even characteristic of the disease.

Many degenerative disorders are characterized by decline in both mental and motor function, although some, like the muscular dystrophies, affect motor function while sparing cognitive abilities. An important psycho-diagnostic consideration involves the segregation of real decline in cognitive function from decline on psychometric measures resulting from motor or sensory impairment. As described in Chapter 3, it is helpful to break down response to a given test item into receptive, associative, and expressive aspects; thereby the relative involvement of each aspect can help clarify a child's difficulty with a given test item. In cases where both cognitive and motor abilities are declining, this can differentiate actual cognitive decline from decline on the ability to perform the motor requirements of the test items, ranging from expressive language to manual dexterity.

Genetic problems present distinct issues from those encountered in degenerative diseases. Whereas the child with degenerative problems, especially those with onset in later childhood years, may have acquired a skill before beginning to lose it, the child with genetic (or very early onset) problems lacks the experiences necessary for the development of a given skill. Performance on many standardized psychometric types of measures assumes the opportunity for interaction with the environment to an extent sufficient for the development of the skill, so that the child with a chronic handicapping condition may appear to be more handicapped than is the case. The child with chronic motor problems that preclude the exercise of normal interactions with toys and motor manipulanda may perform at a spuriously low level on items (e.g., Wechsler Object Assembly), resulting in both an underestimation of potential and the construction of a test profile that suggests false positive neuropsychological impairment.

INTERACTIVE DEFICITS

As mentioned, some childhood diseases such as head trauma or Tourette syndrome may limit the child's abilities to perform on test items involving such components as memory or motor speed. Other childhood diseases, such as epilepsy or hydrocephalus, may have special limiting effects on performance involving concentration, psychomotor function, or nonverbal context. Such deficits may result more directly from medical or surgical treatment than from the disease itself. Therefore as psychologists become involved increasingly in the evaluation of children with neurodevelopmental diseases, they need to know how the diseases (or their treatment) may relate to assessment procedures and findings.

It is presumed that no properly trained psychologist would evaluate a blind child with the WISC-R and fail to recognize the role of vision on Performance scales, nor evaluate a deaf child on the same scale and fail to recognize the role of hearing on the Verbal scale. However, most psychologists may not show comparable expertise in recognizing the possible influences of more subtle, central nervous system impairments on performance on a number of psychometric measures. In the case of a child with mild left visual field neglect due to contralateral cerebral hemisphere impairments, ignoring or misperceiving the left portions of stimuli on such test items as WRAT reading scales could be scored as reading errors. Although technically the resultant reading standard score could be interpreted as a valid estimate of the child's current reading ability (just as a blind child's WISC-R Performance score could be interpreted as representing the child's current functional abilities for such tasks), this obviously would ignore important implications for both etiologic interpretation and the development of appropriate interpretation and programming.

Within the context of possible left-hand misperceptions on fingertip number writing, distortions or comparative neglect of the left side of stimuli on tasks such as design copying, human figure drawing, or Block Design, or with other related clues, such findings can be of value in developing a comprehensive diagnostic profile with many important applications for alleviating problems in daily social and academic contexts. Simple intervention strategies could involve positioning the child in a more facilitative classroom position (i.e., to the left, where the left-sided misperceptions or neglect will have less impact on processing information from blackboard or charts), or teaching the child to focus to the left of materials to be read or studied (so as to help insure that the entire visual context will receive adequate attention).

For a child who has either disease-related (e.g., Tourette syndrome) or treatment-related (e.g., epilepsy) problems with performance on such timed motor tasks as some WISC-R Performance items, recommendations could include de-emphasis on timed academic work. This type of performance may measure the impact of the child's disease (or its treatment) rather than knowledge acquired from instruction. Just as it would be inappropriate to fail a child with hemiplegia on a physical education exam that required running a given distance in a specified time, it is inappropriate to maintain school or parental expectations that are precluded by neurologically mediated handicaps. The psychologist who carefully assesses the functional capacities of such a child can make important contributions to the child's progress in the social and educational milieu by relating examination findings to their implications in non-test settings. This intervention may take the following forms: (a) helping the child, teachers, and parents recognize that poor performance is due to real limitations, (b) helping translate the child's residual functional assets to constructive foci for academic and social skill enhancement, or (c) helping relate the deficits found on assessment to the underlying handicapping condition. In some cases all these may be appropriate, but in other cases similarly relevant data from psychological assessment can be used to ameliorate the effects of the disease on the child's personal, social, and academic development.

Because children's personal, social, and academic development are so interrelated, the child with a neurodevelopmental problem that impairs school performance, for example, may very often experience problems in the development of self-concept and subsequent peer interactions. Therefore it is important to identify the nature and extent of neuropsychological impairments affecting any aspect of the child's functioning so that intervention facilitates the total spectrum of development.

SUMMARY

Neuropsychological evaluation is especially valuable in assessing neurodevelopmental problems in the school-aged child. Many of these children have unique difficulties with sensory, perceptual, associative, or expressive processing. Unless the neuropsychological substrates of such processing are considered, difficulties on given perceptual or expressive tasks may be interpreted as representing (false positive) cognitive handicaps. This could result in the development of unrealistic plans for children that do not take into account their potential abilities.

Each type of neurodevelopmental problem, be it head injury, epilepsy, hydrocephalus, Tourette syndrome, genetic, or degenerative disorder, has unique diagnostic features that may require a unique approach to evaluation. A neuropsychological conceptual approach that considers the various phenomena producing the pattern of findings for a given child allows the psychologist to integrate various physical, intellectual, sensory, and motor findings into a global diagnostic picture with implications for intervention and planning.

REFERENCES

Abuzzahab, F. S., & Anderson, F. O. (1973). Gilles de la Tourette's syndrome. *International Registry Minnesota Medicine, 56,* 492-496.

Alajouanine, T., & Lhermitte, F. (1965). Acquired aphasia in children. *Brain, 88,* 653-662.

Annegers, J. F., Grabow, J. D., Kurland, L. T., & Louis, E. R. (1980). The incidence, causes, secular trends of head trauma in Olmstead County, Minnesota. *Neurology, 30,* 912-919.

Aram, D., Ekelman, B., Rose, D., & Whitaker, H. (1985). Verbal and cognitive sequelae following unilateral lesions acquired in early childhood. *Journal of Clinical and Experimental Neuropsychology, 7,* 55-78.

Benton, A. L. (1979). Behavioral consequences of closed head injury. In G. L. Odem (Ed.), *Central Nervous System Trauma Research Status Report* (pp. 220-231). Bethesda, MD: NINCDS.

Black, P., Jeffries, J., Blumer, D., Wellner, A., & Walker, A. (1969). The post traumatic syndrome in children: characteristics and incidence. In A. Walder, W. Caveness, & M. Critchley (Eds.), *Late Effects of Head Injury* (pp. 142-149). Springfield, IL: C. C. Thomas.

Boll, T. J. (1982). Behavioral sequelae of head injury. In O. R. Cooper (Ed.), *Head Injury* (pp. 363-375). Baltimore: Williams & Wilkins.

Brooks, D. N. (1972). Memory and head injury. *Journal of Nervous and Mental Diseases, 155,* 350-355.

Brooks, D. N. (1974). Recognition memory and head injury. *Journal of Neurology, Neurosurgery and Psychiatry, 37,* 794-801.

Bruce, D., Schut, L., Bruno, L., Woods, J., & Sutton, L. (1978). Outcome following severe head injury in children. *Journal of Neurosurgery, 48,* 679-688.

Caveness, W. (1977). Incidence of cranio-cerebral trauma in the United States. *Transactions of the American Neurological Association, 102,* 136-138.

Cermack, L. A. (1985, February). *The Effects of Age at Onset and Causal Agent of Brain Injury on Later Adaptive Functioning in Children.* Paper presented at International Neuropsychological Society meeting, San Diego.

Cohen, D., Shaywitz, B., Caparulo, B., Young, F., & Bowers, M. (1978). Chronic, multiple tics in Gilles de la Tourette's disease. *Archives of General Psychiatry,* *35,* 245-250.

Comings, D. E., & Comings, B. G. (1985). Tourette's syndrome: Clinical and psychological aspects of 250 cases. *American Journal of Human Genetics, 37,* 435-450.

Conners, C. K. (1982). Parent and teacher rating forms for the assessment of hyperkinesis in children. In P. A. Keller & L. G. Ritt (Eds.), *Innovations in Clinical Practice: A Source Book* (Vol. 1, pp. 257-264). Sarasota, FL: Professional Resource Exchange, Inc.

Craft, A. W. (1972). Head injury in children. In P. J. Vinken & G. W. Bruyn (Eds.), *Handbook of Clinical Neurology* (Vol. 23, pp. 445-458). New York: Elsevier.

Dornbush, M. P. (1984). *Neuropsychological Functioning of School-Age Children with Tourette Syndrome.* Unpublished doctoral dissertation, Georgia State University, Atlanta.

Dornbush, M. P., & Hartlage, L. C. (1984, October). *Dyscalculia in Tourette Syndrome: Fact or Artifact.* Paper presented at National Academy of Neuropsychologists meeting, San Diego.

Dyken, P. R., & Krawiecki, N. (1983). Neurodegenerative diseases in infancy and childhood. *Annals of Neurology, 13*(4), 351-364.

Epilepsy Foundation of America. (1975). *Basic Statistics on the Epilepsies.* Philadelphia: F. A. Davis Co.

Field, J., Corbin, K., Goldstein, N., & Klass, D. (1966). Gilles de la Tourette syndrome. *Neurology, 16,* 453-462.

Gilroy, J., & Meyer, J. S. (1975). *Medical Neurology.* New York: Macmillan.

Goethe, K. E., & Levin, H. S. (1984). Behavioral manifestations during the early and long-term stages of recovery after closed head injury. *Psychiatric Annals, 14,* 540-546.

Golden, G. S. (1979). Tics and Tourette syndrome. *Hospital Practice, 14,* 91-97.

Hannay, H. J., Levin, H., & Grossman, R. (1979). Impaired recognition memory after head injury. *Cortex, 15,* 269-283.

Hartlage, L. C. (1977, February). *Some Psychological Aspects Concerning Patients with Dysraphic Lesions: The Use of Psychometric Examinations in Followup of Patients.* Presented at a conference on Spinal

Dysraphisms and Related Conditions: A Multidisciplinary Approach, Augusta, GA.

Hartlage, L. C. (1981). Neuropsychological assessment of anticonvulsant drug toxicity. *Clinical Neuropsychology, 3,* 20-22.

Hartlage, L. C. (1984, August). *False Positive Lateralizing Signs Related to Anticonvulsant Medication.* Paper presented at American Psychological Association meeting, Toronto.

Hartlage, L. C. (1985, October). *Behavioral Sequelae of Traumatic Head Injury: Pre-Post Checklist.* Paper presented at National Academy of Neuropsychologists meeting, Philadelphia.

Hartlage, L. C., & Green, J. B. (1971). Comparative performance of epileptic and non-epileptic children and adolescents on tests of academic, communications, and social skills. *Diseases of the Nervous System, 32,* 418-421.

Hartlage, L. C., & Green, J. B. (1972). The relationship between parental attitudes and social achievement in epileptic children. *Epilepsia, 13,* 21-26.

Hecaen, H. (1976). Acquired aphasia in children and the ontogenesis of hemispheric functional specialization. *Brain and Language, 3,* 114-134.

Incagnoli, T., & Kane, R. (1981). Neuropsychological functioning in Tourette syndrome. *Advances in Neurology, 35,* 305-310.

Jagger, J., Prusoff, B., Cohen, D., Kidd, K., & Carbonari, C. (1982). The epidemiology of Tourette syndrome: A pilot study. *Schizophrenia Bulletin, 8,* 267-278.

Jennett, B. (1978). The problem of mild head injury. *Practitioner, 221,* 77-82.

Klonoff, H., Low, M., & Clark, C. (1977). Head injuries in children: A prospective five year follow up. *Journal of Neurology, Neurosurgery, and Psychiatry, 40,* 1211-1219.

Laurence, K. M., & Coates, S. (1967). *Spontaneously Arrested Hydrocephalus.* New York: The National Foundation-March of Dimes.

Lenneberg, E. (1967). *Biological Foundations of Language.* New York: Wiley.

Lenneberg, E. H., & Lenneberg, E. (1975). *Foundations of Language Development: A Multidisciplinary Approach.* New York: Academic Press.

Levin, H., Eisenberg, H., Wigg, N., & Kobayashi, K. (1982). Memory and intellectual ability after head injury in children and adolescents. *Neurosurgery, 11,* 668-672.

Livingstone, S. (1972). Epilepsy in infancy, childhood, and adolescence. In B. Wolfman (Ed.), *Manual of Child Psychopathology* (pp. 230-269). New York: McGraw-Hill.

Lorber, J. (1967). Recovery of vision following prolonged blindness in children with hydrocephalus or following pyogenic meningitis. *Clinical Pediatrics, 6,* 699-703.

Marie, P. (1971). *Existe-t-il Chez l'homme des Centres Preformes on Innes du Langage? Questions Neurologiques d'actualite* (M. Cole & M. Cole, Trans.). New York: Hafner. (Original work published 1922)

Matthews, E. S., & Ransohoff, J. (1968). Hydrocephalus. In H. Barnett (Ed.), *Pediatrics* (pp. 847-853). New York: Appleton-Century-Crofts.

McLean, A., Temkin, N., Dikmen, S., & Wyler, A. (1983). The behavioral sequelae of head injury. *Journal of Clinical Neuropsychology, 5,* 361-376.

Power, J. P., & Hartlage, L. C. (1982, October). *Long-Term Neuropsychological Sequelae of Closed Head Injury.* Paper presented at National Academy of Neuropsychologists meeting, Atlanta.

Power, J., & Hartlage, L. (1984, August). *Language Learning Disability and Left Temporal Lobe Damage.* Paper presented at American Psychological Association meeting, Toronto.

Rankin, J., Aram, D., & Horowitz, S. (1981). Language ability in right and left hemiplegic children. *Brain and Language, 12,* 292-306.

Rutherford, W., Merrett, J., & McDonald, J. (1977). Sequelae of concussion caused by minor head injuries. *Lancet, 2,* 1315.

Rutter, M. (1981). Psychological sequelae of brain damage in children. *American Journal of Psychiatry, 138,* 1533-1544.

Schulman, K. (1968). Defects of the closure of the neural plate. In H. L. Barnett (Ed.), *Pediatrics* (pp. 853-859). New York: Appleton-Century-Crofts.

Shapiro, A. K., & Shapiro, E. S. (1982). Tourette syndrome: Clinical aspects, treatment, and etiology. *Seminars in Neurology, 2,* 373-385.

Shapiro, A. K., Shapiro, E. S., Bruun, R. D., & Sweet, R. D. (1978). *Gilles de la Tourette's Syndrome.* New York: Raven Press.

Smith, E. (1974). Influence of site of impact on cognitive impairment persisting long after severe closed head injury. *Journal of Neurology, Neurosurgery, and Psychiatry, 37,* 719-726.

Squire, L., & Slater, P. C. (1975). Forgetting in very long-term memory as assessed by an improved questionnaire technique. *Journal of Experimental Psychology: Human Learning and Memory, 1,* 50-54.

Sutherland, R. J., Kolb, B., Schoer, W., Wishaw, I., & Davies, D. (1982). Neuropsychological assessment of children and adults with Tourette syndrome: A comparison with learning disabilities and schizophrenia. *Advances in Neurology, 35,* 311-322.

Thomsen, I. V. (1977). Verbal learning in aphasic and non-aphasic patients with severe head injuries. *Scandinavian Journal of Rehabilitation Medicine, 9,* 73-77.

Winogren, H., Knights, R., & Bawden, H. (1983, February). *Neuropsychological Deficits Following Head Injury in Children.* Paper presented at International Neuropsychological Society meeting, Mexico City.

Yeni-Komshian, G. H. (1977, April). *Speech Perception in Brain Injured Children.* Paper presented at the conference on the Biological Basis of Delayed Language Development, New York.

6

SPECIAL CONSIDERATIONS REGARDING THE ASSESSMENT OF ADOLESCENTS

INTRODUCTION

By the time a child has reached adolescence, it is likely that most conditions such as learning disorders or other developmental problems will have been recognized, diagnosed, and received some type of treatment or intervention. Thus assessment at this age level is not likely to concern strict diagnostic or classificatory issues in order to provide special education or handicapped children's medical services or to identify short-term educational or social intervention strategies. Rather, assessment of the adolescent is likely to relate to career goals and vocational planning (Hartlage & Telzrow, 1984). It is important at this age to determine whether college, technical training, or entry into the work force is the most appropriate objective. Once general goals have been identified, neuropsychological data can be used to focus on specific aspects of appropriate educational or vocational alternatives. The individual's unique abilities, aspirations, and resources are combined with this information to create a plan for achieving these goals.

ILLUSTRATION OF CAREER GOAL-SETTING FROM NEUROPSYCHOLOGICAL DATA

Assessment of the adolescent does not need to be restricted by specific diagnostic issues (Hartlage &

Telzrow, 1983). Obviously the child with a previously identified neuropsychological problem will require further evaluation during adolescence with regard to future planning and career goals. However, the adolescent without previously determined neuropsychological deficits also can benefit from such assessment in order to identify areas of strength or weakness that affect future career choices.

For example, a child of 17 with well above average mental ability, who has not experienced significant prior educational problems, may have neuropsychological asymmetries of cognitive and psychomotor function that should be considered in establishing realistic career goals. Assume, for example, that this child has a Full Scale IQ of 121, a Verbal IQ of 128, and a Performance IQ of 105, with right-hand sensory and motor functions in the top 5 percentiles and left-hand functions around the 60th percentile, and other psychometric, developmental, and academic functions compatible with this type and extent of asymmetry. Educational or career goals focused toward architecture, dentistry, engineering, or related fields would be much less likely to result in success than educational programs more oriented toward language or verbal skill utilization, such as education, law, or public relations.

Although the obvious factor of global mental ability and the potential implications of such a large V>P IQ discrepancy might suggest such a career choice, it is possible that the child has chosen more verbally oriented courses, which were reflected in the IQ profile. Further academic respecialization might attenuate this V>P discrepancy to some extent. However, when the motor, sensory, developmental, and other psychometric data are consistent with this pattern of abilities, the IQ results may indicate more efficient processing of functions related to the left hemisphere. Therefore educational emphasis on tasks reflected by the Performance IQ would not necessarily change the configuration of mental abilities, with the potential vocational implications of such a change.

This example illustrates how normal variability in neuropsychological organization may be useful in career planning. Research and clinical work in neuropsychology usually has involved handicapped individuals, so we will focus first on how these handicapping conditions relate to adolescence.

THE FRONTAL LOBES

Adolescence in many cases marks the emergence of abilities typically attributed to maturation of the frontal lobes. Although the frontal lobe is usually not fully mature until late adolescence, and often not until age 21 in boys, its maturation is associated with behavioral changes concerning judgment, planning, and realistic assessment of risks and consequences of given behaviors. Frontal lobe function is not directly assessed by most neuropsychological instruments. However, it has unique qualitative features often relevant to assessment and planning with the adolescent.

When a child has sustained brain injury *in utero* or at any subsequent developmental stage, the effects may not become apparent until late adolescence or even slightly beyond. This circumstance is particularly relevant when the assessment for possible neuropsychological injuries involves pending litigation or lawsuit, because frontal lobe injury in childhood may not produce observable effects until adolescence or young adulthood. Thus, when feasible, the development of diagnostic findings for predicting longer term outcomes of possible frontal lobe injury in children may well be postponed until the possible implications of such damage can be assessed more comprehensively. Some frontal lobe injury also may be associated with most closed traumatic head injuries. Obviously a direct blow to the frontal area, such as the head striking a windshield, has clear potential for frontal lobe injury. Similarly, a blow to the rear of the head has clear potential for *contre-coup* injury to the frontal lobe caused by the brain's striking the frontal bone when rebounding from posterior impact. Further, blows to posterior parietal areas of the brain from either side may result in a *contre-coup* trauma to the frontal areas contralateral to the blow. Finally, a lateral blow to one frontal area can result in *contre-coup* damage to the contralateral frontal area.

Some formal neuropsychological measures, such as the Wisconsin Card Sorting Test (WCST) (Heaton, 1981), may help identify frontal lobe injury, but findings from this (or any) single measure must be interpreted carefully because impairments of other brain areas also can affect performance. Common behavioral correlates of frontal lobe injury include social crudity (e.g., belching, nose picking) and inappropriate behaviors (e.g., giggling, yawning) that, although by no means uncommon among adolescents nor diagnostic by themselves, tend to be more frequent and pronounced following frontal injury. Impulsiveness, another common feature of frontal lobe damage, may be noted on the child's approach to test items: For example, blurting out obviously incorrect or irrelevant responses that, on questioning or spontaneous retraction by the child, represent items for which the child knows the correct response. Again, although not specifically diagnostic, in the context of the adolescent child's global behavior such characteristics can help identify a frontal lobe problem. Occasionally noted are dysphorias, in the form of either inappropriate euphoria or elation, or apparent pressured speech. As with most other indices of frontal lobe impairment, however, such indicators need to be interpreted within the total context of the child's behavior.

When impairment to frontal cortical areas involves posterior frontal areas, motor functions may be affected. Examples include bilateral slowing on initial rate of rapid finger oscillation, or unilateral slowing corresponding to the contralateral side of damage. Frontal motor impairment also can be detected by difficulty with executing the motoric aspects of such tasks as design copying, when the child recognizes poor performance but cannot improve on it. Occasionally, central dysarthric language problems may suggest frontal lobe impairment. Usually related to left frontal lobe damage, dysarthria also may result from bilateral or right frontal damage. Typically, expressive language facility on articulatory, word finding, or verbal fluency tasks will be somewhat lower than other aspects (e.g., receptive) of language when the damage affects primarily frontal lobe function.

Although hard neurologic findings are confirmatory, by no means will frontal lobe damage always be verifiable by CT or EEG findings. An adolescent with convincing behavioral and neuropsychological evidence of frontal lobe impairment may well have negative findings on such neuroradiologic or electrophysiological studies (Levin, Eisenberg, Wigg, & Kobayashi, 1982). Neuropsychological assessment focusing on functions mediated by the frontal lobes provides very sensitive indicators of such dysfunction to a greater extent than structural or physiological measures. Frequently, adolescent victims of falls or automotive injuries may be examined, treated, and released from hospitals without medical evidence of impairment. However, subsequently these youngsters may be described by parents or teachers as having undergone significant personality changes, such as those described above. Such adolescents may well benefit from careful neuropsychological assessment for the purpose of determining frontal lobe etiology to such changes.

Although frontal lobe injury can occur at any age, adolescence represents the highest incidence period, with adolescent boys at special risk. Thus in the adolescent child, consideration of possible frontal lobe etiology of academic or behavior problems, with the potential implications of such impairment for subsequent planning, is especially relevant.

LEARNING DISORDERS IN ADOLESCENCE

Although most learning disorders will have been diagnosed and, we hope, treated in childhood, they tend to persist into adolescence and beyond. As mentioned earlier, assessment of the learning disabled adolescent focuses on career planning rather than the determination of eligibility for services or planning for the nature of such services, as for younger children. However, the same neuropsychological assessment model can, with a few modifications, provide data equally relevant to the needs of the adolescent.

There is increasing recognition of the importance of assessment in planning for the learning disabled adolescent. Whereas early pressures from parent groups and teacher organizations emphasized services and programs for the younger child, during the last decade strong pressure from such groups has focused attention on the learning disabled adolescent (Johnson, 1984; Lerner, 1981). As Lerner (1981) has observed, in many cases the only common trait shared by adolescents with learning disabilities is a discrepancy between apparent ability and actual academic achievement. Although such a characteristic also could be applied to younger children with learning disabilities, by adolescence the heterogeneity is much more pronounced. Such children have had more time to differentiate on the basis of social and personal exposures and traits, respectively. Further, some of the more homogeneous characteristics common to segments of younger LD children, such as hyperactivity, may tend to resolve at puberty. Finally, the interaction of changing neuropsychological status, as in frontal lobe maturation, and emotional phenomena related to adolescence, can create differences from younger children with learning problems bearing the same label. By adolescence, the cumulative effects of chronic school difficulty may be reflected in depressed self-esteem, which only compounds the difficulties common to most adolescents.

Although the multiple problems associated with learning disabilities during adolescence are being recognized, it is sometimes difficult to identify such children. Unlike the situation in primary grades, where the curriculum is typically invariant, the LD adolescent may be able to select courses in which his or her learning problems are less manifest. This may help account for a widespread but undocumented belief that many children with learning disabilities tend to "outgrow" them. As mentioned, a neuropsychological assessment model usually will help pull together a profile of the LD adolescent's assets and problems so that appropriate educational and career goals can be identified, and strategies developed for accomplishing these goals can be employed.

Developmental history for the adolescent can be replaced by educational history, to focus on which courses, subject matter, and study or examination approaches have been comparatively easy or comparatively difficult. Such patterns as special difficulty (or facility) in reading, calculating, spatial relationships, or music, for example, may provide clues concerning potential career or future educational problems or strengths. Study approaches that were comparatively helpful (or nonproductive) also can provide important information. Did the student learn better by memorizing words, or by visual cues? What types of examination formats (independent of subject matter) were comparatively easy or difficult? Were written or verbal expression examination formats more difficult than multiple-choice, matching, or true-false?

The LD adolescent who has consistent problems with language - reading and language usage, verbal or written expression - may exhibit generalized left cerebral hemisphere problems, which can be tested by appropriate neuropsychological measures. Given a P>V IQ profile, Beery VMI>PPVT, and left-hand superiority on motor and sensory measures, this hypothesis becomes more tenable. Possible strengths in music and spatial relationships may suggest compensating right hemisphere abilities, which may be reflected in better performance on tests using true-false, matching, or multiple-choice formats. Difficulty memorizing words and better success in visualization memory would be compatible with such findings and would help identify both possible career pitfalls and potentials, as well as suggest ways in which learning for further educational or job preparation might be enhanced.

An obvious first level of interpretive inference is the global IQ level. Although the IQ was originally developed as a means for predicting school success, there are some general guidelines for relating IQ to potential vocational level (Hartlage & Lucas, 1973). Typically, IQ values below 70 are associated with sheltered employment and some unskilled labor, such as migrant farm work or routine, repetitive work like simple assembly or manual labor tasks. In the 70-80 IQ range, a fairly wide variety of unskilled, nonjudgmental manual labor tasks, and some porter, janitorial, housekeeping, and child-care jobs, as well as simple assembly and inspecting jobs, are feasible. The 80-90 IQ range may be compatible with some semiskilled work, such as equipment operation, truck driving, and a wide range of factory work in many industries. The 90-100 IQ range is compatible with a number of trades, such as painting, welding, and fire fighting, as well as typing, filing, and most entry level secretarial jobs. Intelligence quotient values between 100 and 110 are compatible with most skilled trades, with potential for small business operation and higher level clerical and sales positions. Their level of mental ability also may be reflected in graduation from junior college, technical school, or earning associate college degrees, or completing training for such activities as diverse as practical nursing or technician work. The 110-120 IQ range is that typically associated with successful completion of baccalaureate college level work, promotion to supervisory levels, or success in private enterprise as an owner-manager. For those individuals fortunate enough to fall in the IQ range 120 and above, proficiencies in the college graduate level occupations and success in graduate education and the professions may be feasible career goals.

Following the development of a range of career goals compatible with level of global mental ability, the next step in relating assessment findings to career possibilities can involve looking at measures of abilities sensitive to facility or difficulty in the processing of verbal versus spatial types of information. At any given intellectual level, this can provide important clues for initial specialization within that ability level. In general, adolescents at any intellectual level who display consistent superiority in verbally mediated tasks and consistently poorer performance on spatially mediated tasks are more likely to do well in careers that emphasize verbal over spatial facility. In the upper IQ ranges, these might suggest success in fields such as law, psychiatry, or psychology, as opposed to engineering, surgery, or architecture. In the 110-120 IQ range, careers such as teaching, selling, or announcing might be more viable than drafting, designing, or mechanical specializations. In the 100-110 IQ range, copy writing, sales, or other public contact work might be more feasible than a skilled trade such as electrician, artisan, or repair work. From 90-100 IQ, secretarial, receptionist, or retail clerk work represent more successful career goals than painting, fire fighting, or semiskilled trades work. Individuals with IQ levels below 90 have more limited vocational and career options, but again consideration of language versus spatial facilities may help differentiate between poor inspector or assembler potential and greater success in more verbally specialized work areas such as public service (e.g., nursing aide, companion, or telephone answering service).

Although there is no assurance that such differentiation will result in career goal realization, it is generally recognized that people are more productive and better satisfied in work that suits their talents and abilities, thus helping to maximize the likelihood of a satisfying career choice. Assume, for example, that an adolescent age 17 with a Full Scale IQ of 130, who has been diagnosed as having a visual-perceptual type of learning disability, has a Verbal IQ of 136 with a Performance IQ of 108. All developmental and educational history reports, and motor, sensory, and psychometric measures, suggest consistent facility in processing the sorts of information more efficiently processed by the left cerebral hemisphere. This adolescent, whose father and mother are both surgeons, wants a similar career in medicine. A Full Scale IQ of 130 is somewhat above that of average entering medical students, and assuming adequate motivation and appropriate study habits, suggests a fairly good likelihood of success in handling the academic content of medical school. Study habits oriented toward verbal rehearsal, as opposed to visual recall, represent helpful approaches. In terms of career planning, medical specialties such as surgery, which require high levels of visuo-spatial facility, would not be practical, whereas the likelihood of success in more verbal medical specialties such as psychiatry or certain types of medical education is comparatively good.

Once career goals have been identified, whether or not post-secondary education or training is indicated, neuropsychological findings can be applied to specific curricular choices. The child with defective language processing and other left hemisphere mediated ability may be able to select courses with comparatively less emphasis on these abilities, such as home economics, vocational training, music, physical and driver education, and art. Even in a college preparatory course, some curricular alternatives may be feasible for such a child. Some subjects, such as physics and geometry, lend themselves more readily to right hemisphere processing strategies than others, and may be utilized to meet core requirements in math or science groupings. Even in courses requiring heavy involvement of deficit areas, it may be possible to translate neuropsychological findings into study approaches. If, for example, a health course requires learning the cranial nerves, a left hemisphere strategy could use mnemonic memorization clues, such as "On Old Olympus' Towering Top" to help cue the names of cranial nerves 1-5 (i.e., olfactory, optic, oculomotor, trochlear, trigeminal). A right hemisphere strategy for this same task could involve a visual diagram, with the names written on the nerves in such a way that visual memory cues are activated.

With special neuropsychological learning deficits, such as dyslexia or dyscalculia, the translation into career alternatives is fairly obvious. The child with dyslexia obviously would experience considerable difficulty in any career involving fairly fluent reading. Even some jobs that do not obviously require reading may present problems: Inability to read instructions concerning machine operation or cleaning materials, for example, could interfere with success in mechanical or janitorial work.

Similarly, the adolescent with dyscalculia probably should avoid fields like accounting, or even some business careers where calculation is important. If severe, such a problem can preclude even simple clerical jobs that involve making change. With respect to relating academic skill levels to function, a third-grade math facility will probably suffice for simple change making, and a third-grade reading level may suffice for reading comics or very simple directions.   An eighth-grade level math ability will suffice for most routine record keeping, and an eighth-grade level reading ability is generally adequate for reading all parts of a newspaper and most common directions (except for those on income tax forms!).   The translation of adolescent neuropsychological test findings into career planning thus requires some knowledge of both neuropsychology and the demands of various jobs. In most cases specialists in each area can collaborate to develop an optimum match between the adolescent and a family of occupations appropriate to his or her unique neuropsychological profile.

Because many learning disabled adolescents hope to pursue college work, a number of colleges have developed special programs for such individuals.   In 1981, Vogel and Adelman published a description and listing of college and university programs for the learning disabled, and since that time a number of other such programs have been developed.   College is now a very viable alternative for individuals with adequate global mental ability who have even moderately severe learning disabilities in some spheres.   The same sorts of curricular decisions and study approaches that were outlined above are applicable to the LD college student as well.

NEURODEVELOPMENTAL
HANDICAPS IN ADOLESCENCE

Although most neurodevelopmental problems manifest before adolescence, the impact of their handicapping effects peaks during the adolescent years.   Problems such as mental retardation, for example, usually are addressed by public and school agencies during childhood, so that the longer term implications of the handicap do not present as much urgency.   When the child reaches adolescence, however, and approaches the age when public educational systems no longer have programs or mandates for providing services, the individual's total profile of handicaps and possible assets needs to be evaluated in order to develop a plan for the future.

The adolescent with mild mental retardation who has no specific motor or physical limitations other than those related to retarded psychomotor development presents a quite different picture with respect to longer term planning than one who also has motor, sensory, or other deficits. Assuming educational progress at a rate commensurate with mental ability, the 16-year-old adolescent with IQ 65 may be expected to have reading and calculation skills at approximately the third-grade level, and thus may have potential for performing a variety of simple, unskilled tasks, provided there are no compelling physical limitations to performing such tasks. For example, jobs involving packing, assembly, track-feeding, or track take-off activities may be possible, because many such unskilled jobs exist in most areas. Neuropsychological evaluation addressing such relevant issues as fine motor dexterity (e.g., as measured by rate of rapid finger oscillation) or more gross motor coordination (e.g., as measured by the Minnesota Rate of Manipulation Test) can be of value in determining whether such goals are reasonable. Measures of eye-hand coordination, such as design copying, Wechsler Coding or Digit Symbol, Object Assembly, and Block Design scales, also may be relevant. If the individual's Full Scale IQ of 65 consists of Verbal Scale items somewhat above that level, with special impairments on Performance Scale items, the individual may be capable of jobs such as usher, ticket taker, or even cashier in a theatre or similar setting, because the vocational demands would be within such a profile of abilities and handicaps.

In the event motor problems are present to a more pronounced degree in an adolescent with mild mental retardation, competitive employment still can be a possible goal, providing residual functional capacities and limitations revealed on neuropsychological evaluation are considered. Even though work involving such dexterity, be it in assembly, packing, or ticket taking, may be precluded by significant motor or eye-hand impairments in conjunction with mental retardation (such, for example, as might be found in some cases of cerebral palsy or hydrocephalus), examination of test data may reveal possible vocationally relevant assets. The adolescent with mild mental retardation combined with motor or eye-hand impairments who performs relatively well on such tasks as Picture Completion may be capable of some unskilled inspection work, such as the recognition of a defective part or incomplete assembly or packing work.

Through careful consideration of the adolescent's residual assets that may have future vocational relevance, assessment can provide clues to work potential. Appropriate work can be the source of considerable personal satisfaction and sense of accomplishment to the impaired individual. It may be relevant to note that the Social Security Administration does not consider an adolescent or young adult with IQ between 55 and 70 to be disabled, unless an additional handicap imposes further restriction on work potential. Even in cases where the residual functional capacities may not be sufficient for competitive employment, sheltered workshop placement can provide similar satisfaction.

Individuals who are less mentally handicapped by neurodevelopmental disorders have a considerably broader range of vocational options. An adolescent of average or above mental ability with visuo-spatial deficit, although not likely to succeed in careers requiring such abilities, nonetheless has a wide range of career options. Such individuals (who have marked spatial or motor impairments) often succeed in highly verbal careers and as skilled artisans, tradesmen, or repair specialists despite limited verbal skills. Using the sorts of conceptual approaches previously described, it is usually possible to help adolescents with given types and severities of neurodevelopmental problems generate career goals related to their residual functional capacities, in whatever areas and at whatever levels these capacities may be.

A final issue involves avocational planning. By adolescence, individuals have at least begun to develop interests in leisure activities that are, in many cases, related to activities in vogue with peers rather than suited to their own talents or potential abilities. The adolescent with a neurodevelopmental handicap is at considerable risk of frustration and failure unless such activities are chosen with respect to both interest and ability. The levels of concentration required for successful performance on some popular table games may be beyond the capabilities of the adolescent with attention deficit disorder or residual concentration deficits following head injury, for example, and therefore could prove both frustrating and socially unrewarding. The adolescent with visuo-spatial deficits, which might result from nondominant hemisphere damage, dysfunction, or dysgenesis, may experience significant problems with many athletic hobbies requiring average or above average visuo-spatial ability. For such an adolescent, retreat to nonathletic activities such as jigsaw puzzles, crewel, macramé, or related craft activities that depend on this same neuropsychological substrate of behavior may prove equally frustrating, leaving the individual with a sense of not being able to succeed at anything. However, a wide variety of alternative leisure activities could be rewarding and satisfying, provided they focus on assets or areas of strength. If verbal abilities are relatively intact, such activities as scouting projects in areas like citizenship, crossword puzzles, and anagrams may be good alternatives.

For the adolescent with a neurodevelopmental handicap, avocational activities can be especially valuable for providing a sense of accomplishment and self-worth. In many cases the cognitive and social problems associated with such a handicap can preclude some of the normal satisfactions that most other individuals receive in the academic and social context of school. Without guidance, the handicapped adolescent may choose leisure activities that may present further evidence of the handicap at a time when feelings of competence are especially important. By a thoughtful match of assessment findings, using similar strategies and conceptual approaches appropriate for developing career goals, the psychologist can be of considerable help by applying test findings toward the identification of avocational and leisure activities that are appropriate to the adolescent's functional capacities.

SUMMARY

From a neuropsychological perspective, adolescence represents a time of both professional challenge and unique opportunity for making important contributions to long-term planning and the development of career goals. Special professional challenges arise from the need to take findings from such diverse sources as current assessment and educational history and relate them to curricular or training alternatives with given vocational (or avocational) goals. For many years procedures for integrating the findings from neuropsychological assessment and other data sources into psychoeducational or psychodiagnostic profiles for intervention with younger children in school settings have been available. However, few guidelines or procedures for serving adolescents have been available. The unique opportunity arises from the potential for using available data to help the adolescent conceptualize his or her individual constellation of abilities, weaknesses, and special characteristics into a strategy for maximizing strengths and minimizing weaknesses in curricular and career planning. On a short-term basis, this may take the form of planning which courses or training to pursue (or avoid). On a longer term basis, consideration of general career fields and job training strategies may be derived from neuropsychological assessment.

REFERENCES

Hartlage, L. C., & Lucas, D. G. (1973). *Mental Development Evaluation of the Pediatric Patient.* Springfield, IL: Charles C. Thomas.

Hartlage, L. C., & Telzrow, C. F. (1983). The neuropsychological basis of educational intervention. *Journal of Learning Disabilities, 16,* 521-528.

Hartlage, L. C., & Telzrow, C. F. (1984). A neuropsychological model for vocational planning for learning disabled students. In W. Cruickshank & J. Kliebhan (Eds.), *Early Adolescence to Early Adulthood* (pp. 143-156). Syracuse: Syracuse University Press.

Heaton, R. K. (1981). *Wisconsin Card Sorting Test Manual.* Odessa, FL: Psychological Assessment Resources.

Johnson, C. L. (1984). The learning disabled adolescent and young adult: An overview and critique of current practices. *Journal of Learning Disabilities, 17,* 386-391.

Lerner, J. (1981). *Learning Disabilities: Theories, Diagnosis, and Teaching Strategies.* Boston: Houghton-Mifflin.

Levin, H. S., Eisenberg, H. M., Wigg, N. R., & Kobayashi, K. (1982). Memory and intellectual ability after head injury in children and adolescents. *Neurosurgery, 11,* 668-672.

Vogel, S. A., & Adelman, P. (1981). College and university programs designed for learning disabled adults. *Illinois Council for Exceptional Children Quarterly, 30,* 12-18.

APPENDIX:
ADDRESSES OF TEST PUBLISHERS
CITED IN TABLES 1 AND 2

Academic Therapy Publications, 20 Commercial Boulevard, Novato, CA 94947-6191.

American Guidance Services, Publishers' Building, Circle Pines, MN 55014-1796.

Behavior Science Systems, Inc., Box 1108, Minneapolis, MN 55440.

Consulting Psychologists Press, Inc., 577 College Avenue, Palo Alto, CA 94306.

CTB/McGraw-Hill, Del Monte Research Park, Monterey, CA 93940.

Devereux Foundation Press, 19 S. Waterloo Road, Devon, PA 19333.

DLM-Teaching Resources, One DLM Park, Allen, TX 75002.

Follett Publishing Co., 4506 Northwest Highway, Crystal Lake, IL 60014.

Grune & Stratton, Inc., 111 Fifth Avenue, New York, NY 10003.

Charles E. Merrill Publishing Co., 1300 Alum Creek Drive, Box 508, Columbus, OH 43216.

Neuropsychology Press, 1338 East Edison Street, Tucson, AZ 85719.

PRO-ED, 5341 Industrial Oaks Boulevard, Austin, TX 78735.

Psychological Assessment Resources, P. O. Box 98, Odessa, FL 33556.

The Psychological Corp., 555 Academic Court, San Antonio, TX 78204.

Psychological Development Publications, P. O. Box 3198, Aspen, CO 81612.

Reitan Neuropsychology Laboratory, 1338 East Edison Street, Tucson, AZ 87519.

The Riverside Publishing Co., 8420 Bryn Mawr Avenue, Chicago, IL 60631.

Stoelting Co., 1350 S. Kostner Avenue, Chicago, IL 60623.

University Associates in Psychiatry, One South Prospect Street, Burlington, VT 05401.

University Park Press, 233 East Redwood Street, Baltimore, MD 21202.

GLOSSARY

Anoxia. Insufficient supply of oxygen to the body's tissues, which may occur at birth or as a result of trauma or exposure to toxic substances. Anoxia may result in damage to the brain or central nervous system.

Anterior. A directional term that refers to the front portion of the organism.

Attention Deficit Disorder (ADD). A condition of presumed neurologic etiology characterized by unusual difficulty in concentrating and sustaining attention. ADD may occur with or without hyperactivity.

Constructional Praxis. A neurologic deficit resulting in difficulty integrating motor movements to construct (e.g., replicate a block pattern) or copy (e.g., draw or copy geometrical figures).

Contralateral. Literally, "opposite side"; a term which refers to the brain-behavior relationship wherein the left cerebral hemisphere controls the right side of the body for cortical motor and sensory functions.

Coprolalia. Outbursts of a type of obscene language, which may accompany Gilles de la Tourette syndrome.

Dominant. A term used to denote the locus of language; traditionally, the left cerebral hemisphere is referred to as the dominant hemisphere. Also may be used to describe a hand preference.

Dysarthria. A neurologically based disorder of articulation in speech.

Dyscalculia. A neurologically based disorder that impairs one's ability to perform mathematical calculations.

Dyseidetic Dyslexia. A relatively rare type of dyslexia characterized by over-reliance on phonetic cues and visuospatial errors in reading and spelling. Also known as visuo-spatial dyslexia.

Dysgraphia. A neurologic disorder that impairs one's ability to express ideas through writing or written symbols.

Dyslexia. A neurologic disorder that impairs one's ability to read. Spelling typically is impaired as well.

Dysphasia. General term used to refer to language disorders of presumed neurologic origin. Characteristics may include weaknesses in auditory discrimination for speech sounds or delayed or atypical development of speech.

Dysphonetic Dyslexia. The most common type of dyslexia characterized by poor sound-symbol associations, difficulties in sound blending, and auditory discrimination problems. Also known as auditory-phonetic dyslexia.

Dysphoria. A negative affective state.

Echolalia. The repetition of a word or phrase just spoken by another individual. This symptom may be observed in children with neurologic impairment, including those with mental retardation, childhood dysphasia, and Gilles de la Tourette syndrome.

False Negative. Refers to the situation when a negative diagnosis is made and a positive condition actually exists. For example, when a youngster is identified as being free of neurologic disease even though such disease actually is present.

False Positive. Refers to the situation when a positive diagnosis is made and a negative condition actually exists. For example, when a youngster is identified as having a neurologic disease although none is present.

Hemiparesis. Refers to a weakness affecting one side of the body. Hemiparesis may indicate impairment of the central nervous system (e.g., cerebrovascular accident).

Lateral. A directional term that indicates a position away from the midplane, or out toward the side.

Meningomyelocele. A form of spina bifida characterized by an abnormal protrusion of the spinal cord through an opening in the back of the spine.

Morbidity. A state of disease or pathology.

Motor Cortex. Refers to the motor strip located in the posterior portion of the frontal cortex, responsible for cortically controlled motor movement.

Nondominant. Historically, the nondominant hemisphere is the right hemisphere, or the hemisphere not associated with language. The nondominant hand is the nonpreferred hand.

Palilalia. Repetition of one's own words or sounds.

Pathognomonic. Refers to distinctive signs of pathology. For example, a pathognomonic sign on the Aphasia Screening Test is an error typically made only by aphasic persons.

Perceptual Organization. Abilities sensitive to visuospatial skills, such as might be demonstrated by performance on block design and figure copying tests.

Physical Anomalies. Physical malformations which may be minor or severe and which may indicate the presence of a specific syndrome (e.g., Down's syndrome) or central nervous system impairment.

Plasticity. A term used to define the ability of the organism, particularly the young organism, to recover from central nervous system trauma. The degree to which this is possible in the human organism continues to be debated.

Posterior. A directional term that refers to the back of the organism.

Pre-Morbid. Refers to the state of the individual prior to the onset of disease or trauma. Establishing levels of pre-morbid functioning is critical for determining the loss of function as a result of central nervous system trauma.

Sensory Cortex. Refers to the sensory strip, located in the anterior portion of the parietal lobe, responsible for cortically controlled analysis of sensation.

Shunting. A procedure used to drain excess cerebrospinal fluid from the ventricles of the brain in conditions such as hydrocephalus. The shunt (ventriculo-peritoneal shunt) is a narrow plastic tubing inserted into the lateral ventricle, connected to a second tube that drains the fluid from the ventricles into the abdominal cavity.

Subcortical. Describes brain structures located below the cerebral cortex. Such brain regions may be less implicated than cortical structures in higher cognitive processes, but may be critical for such survival functions as respiration and temperature control, as well as for some higher functions such as memory and emotional behavior.

Visuo-Spatial. A type of processing ability typically localized in the right cerebral hemisphere. Visuo-spatial skills may be assessed by performance on block design and form copying tasks.

INDEX